Arduino Without Prior Knowledge

Create your own first project within 7 days

Benjamin Spahic

Content

Introduction

1. Introduction

In 1941, the world was in ruins, but two German engineers presented an invention that has influenced our lives more than any other discovery at the time. We are talking about the "Zuse Z3", the world's first digital computer. Of course, the Zuse Z3 does not compare to today's computers, neither in its construction nor in its technical functionality or its spatial dimensions.

The Zuse Z3 weighs several tons and fills up almost an entire room. At the same time, its computing power is much lower than that of a contemporary pocket calculator. Nevertheless, it is considered a milestone in computer research.

Figure 0 Replica of the Zuse Z3 in the German Museum Munich

The Zuse Z3 was destroyed during the Second World War. When its inventor Konrad Zuse was drafted for the war, he left it behind with the words:

> *"Others leave their family behind, I leave Z3."*

-Konrad Zuse

Introduction

Massive changes have been going on since Zuse Z3, one revolution chased the next. In 1946, the US military introduced ENIAC, the first fully electronic computer. At the same time, the Zuse Z4, the successor to the Z3, is put into operation.

Over time, the computing power has multiplied. While the Zuse Z3 had only 600 computing units (relays), a modern processor has several billion computing units (transistors) within an area of 200 mm². At the same time, the power consumption (power consumption) has decreased considerably.

This technical progress enables us to live life as we do. We work with screens, scroll through social media apps on our smartphones and watch TV series or movies in the evening.

Digitization was, and still is, the greatest revolution in modern history. We have infinite possibilities, but there is a serious lack of enthusiasm in our society. Everybody uses technology and benefits from its progress, but few have the will to understand electrical engineering and programming and to become a part of the invention.

But since you bought this book, you seem to be interested in exactly this topic. This leads us to the core of this book – the Arduino. The Arduino platform is perfect for implementing your own projects, getting to know microcontrollers as well as programming and awakening the spirit of discovery.

Maybe you are a student and strive to program your own robot, maybe you are a skilled programmer who wants to learn more about the hardware, or a young-at-heart pensioner interested in microcontrollers and their programming in general.

In any case, you will not regret learning about the matter.

Certainly, there are many websites and books out there that introduce you to the Arduino theme. However, some of these books are more than 500 pages long and completely unsuitable for newcomers.

Introduction

If you are already familiar with the subject matter and need clues for a specific project, these books can be helpful, but for the majority of interested parties they are neither necessary nor effective.

This particular problem is the reason why this book came into being.

It is a beginners' guide for those who are curious and want to understand the basic principles of the Arduino platform quickly and without substantial prior knowledge. It is intended for everyone who wants to start their first project as soon as possible.

What is a microcontroller anyway? How do I correctly connect sensors and other components to the microcontroller? How do I program quickly and efficiently? All this is worked out step by step and complemented with a real example project.

Prerequisites and level of knowledge:

This book is suitable for anyone with a basic enthusiasm for technology and programming. Basic knowledge of physics, for example calculating with SI units, is important and will therefore be summarized.

Furthermore, knowing the basics of electrical engineering will help you understand more complex circuit diagrams and current flows.

Since some readers might not have any experience with the programming language "C/C#" or with electronic circuits and components, the first chapter deals with the basics of C programming and electrical engineering. However, this book only covers the necessary basics. If you want to gain more in-depth knowledge, for example in programming, it is recommended that you consult further literature about this topic.

Thus, this book is intended for readers with technical basics but without a deeper knowledge of Arduino.

If you feel competent in these areas, you can start with the third chapter, which deals specifically with the Arduino platform and different versions of microcontrollers. However, it is recommended to at least review the basics.

The following icons will lead you through the book:

Introduction

 Calculation symbols: This is where we discuss more complex aspects in excursuses or derivations. The derivation of a topic might broaden your understanding, but is not essential and rather intended for reference.

 Light Bulb: Here, the main points of a chapter are summarized. These statements are well suited for reference or when you skim over a specific topic again.

 Attention: Frequent errors are mentioned here. This area shows where and why obstacles or false assumptions might occur.

 Calculator: Sample calculations or questions for comprehension and internalization.

Now I wish you a lot of fun reading about and immersing yourself in the Arduino ecosystem.

2. Fundamentals of Electrical Engineering

The Arduino platform combines hardware and software. To use the Arduino ecosystem in a meaningful way, you must understand circuits and peripherals in the form of components. Therefore, we will first look at the physical quantities current, voltage, power, and energy. These are known to everyone, but are often misused or misinterpreted.

The following definitions are based on the book "Electrical Engineering without prior knowledge – Understanding the basics in 7 days." The book completes the book series and is equally beginner-friendly as this book.

If you want to build a fundamental understanding of electrical engineering, I recommend reading this guidebook, too.

2.1. Electrical Potential φ

Electrical potential, also called electrostatic potential, is abbreviated with φ (Greek small letter Phi). It has the unit volt V.

 Electrical potential describes the potential energy of a test charge within an electrical field. The electric field assigns a potential to every point in space.

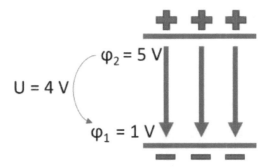

Figure 1 Potentials and voltage in the homogeneous E-field

2.2. Voltage U

The difference between two potentials $\varphi_2 - \varphi_1$ is called voltage U, the voltage also has the unit volt V.

 Always make sure that a voltage only indicates a potential difference. Therefore, a reference potential is always required.

A normal battery has a voltage of 1.5 V. This means that the positive pole, i. e. the upper contact point of the battery, has an electrical potential that is 1.5 V higher than the negative pole.

2.3. Current I

A measure for the strength of the electron flow is the current, abbreviated with the symbol I. Its unit is ampere A.

 In the technical circuit, the current always flows from the positive pole to the negative pole, although the electrons physically flow from the negative pole to the positive pole.

2.4. Energy E and Power P

2.4.1. Energy

The terms energy and work are used for the same physical quantity. Energy, or also the performed work, is abbreviated with E or W.

Energy indicates how much work a system is capable of, for example how much heat it can generate. Energy is independent from time. Its SI-unit is the joule J.

Alternative units are watt seconds Ws or kilowatt hours kWh. Naturalized units for energy are, for example, kilocalories kcal.

Fundamentals of Electrical Engineering

Energy Conservation:

 Conservation of energy means that there is a fixed amount of energy in the universe and that this energy cannot be destroyed or generated. Energy can only be converted into different forms.

2.4.2. Power P

 Power, on the other hand, is a physical quantity and refers to the energy or work that is converted in a certain time.

$$P = \frac{\Delta E}{\Delta t}$$

The unit of power is the watt, corresponding to energy per time. The unit of energy is the joule, the unit of time is the second.

One watt corresponds to one joule per second $1\frac{J}{s} = 1W$

 The electrical power that is converted into systems or components is calculated by multiplying the applied voltage by the current.

$$P = U \cdot I$$

2.5. Resistor R

 Electrical resistance is, as the name suggests, a resistance for electrons. It makes it more difficult for electrons to flow through the resistor.

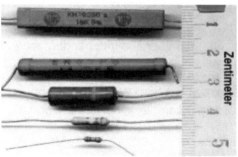

Figure 2 Different types of resistors

Electrical resistance has the symbol R and is given in ohm Ω.

8

Fundamentals of Electrical Engineering

💡 Electric resistance indicates the electric voltage U, which is needed to let a current I flow through an electric conductor.

$$R = \frac{U}{I}$$

The unit ohm is therefore $1\Omega = \frac{1V}{1A}$

We can change the formulas accordingly to

$$U = R \cdot I$$

💡 A mnemonic that indicates the relationship between voltage, resistance and current in a circuit is therefore "URI".

The resistor is also an electrical component. When we speak of a resistor, we usually mean the concrete component.

The circuit symbol is drawn as a rectangle.

Figure 3 American circuit symbol   *European circuit symbol*

2.5.1. Voltage Divider

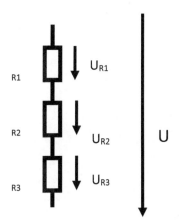

We have several resistors connected in a series and know the voltage that drops across all resistors together. But how much voltage drops across the individual resistors?

9

The resistors divide the voltage among themselves in proportion to their resistance values and thus form a voltage divider.

$$\frac{Voltage\ at\ resistor}{Total\ voltage} = \frac{Resistance\ value}{Total\ resistance}$$

$$U_{R1} = U_0 \cdot \frac{R_1}{R_1 + R_2 + R_3 + \cdots}$$

$$U_{R2} = U_0 \cdot \frac{R_2}{R_1 + R_2 + R_3 + \cdots}$$

$$\cdots$$

$$U_0 = 10V, R_1 = 6\Omega, R_2 = 4\Omega$$

$$U_{R1} = 10V \cdot \frac{6\Omega}{6\Omega + 4\Omega} = 6V$$

$$U_{R2} = 10V \cdot \frac{4\Omega}{6\Omega + 4\Omega} = 4V$$

2.6. The Diode

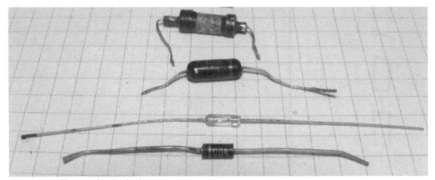

Figure 1 Different diode designs

A diode is a component that allows the current to pass in one direction only. This is why it is also called a semiconductor component.

Figure 2 Diode circuit symbol

The diode consists of an anode, which is connected to the positive pole or the higher potential, and a cathode, which is connected to the negative pole or the lower potential.

 A vertical line on the component indicates which wire represents the cathode.

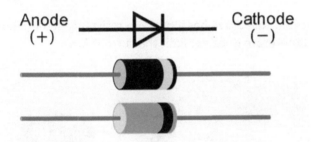

Figure 3 Anode and cathode of a diode

 Because the diode only conducts in one direction, we speak of operating the diode either in flow direction or in reverse direction.

Approximately 0.7 V drop in flow direction at a standard silicon diode. A Schottky diode, for example, only conducts 0.2 V.

 A diode has almost no resistance in flow direction and therefore does not limit the current flow. You will need another resistor, otherwise you risk creating a practical short circuit. This is called a series resistor.

Excursus: LED

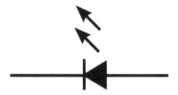

Figure 4Switching symbol LED

The mode of operation and characteristics of a light-emitting diode are the same as those of a "normal" semiconductor diode.

However, LEDs usually have a higher forward voltage of about 1.6 V - 2.6 V instead of 0.7 V.

! Even a light-emitting diode has almost no resistance in direction of flow and therefore does not limit the current flow.

2.7. The Capacitor and Capacitance C

Figure 5 Various capacitors

Similar to a battery, the capacitor has the ability to store electrical charges, but for shorter periods of time.

They are, therefore, perfectly suited to support voltages and currents. If a voltage source cannot provide the required amount of current, the capacitor serves as a buffer storage, so to speak.

If required, they can release a lot of energy in a short time. Afterwards, when the load is low, they recharge again.

Such capacitors are almost always installed parallelly to supply voltages to support them. This is why they are also called support capacitors.

The constant, which indicates the relation between voltage and charge, is called capacity C. Its unit is the farad F.

 In reality, the capacitances of capacitors are relatively small. The order of magnitude of capacitance is in the micro, nano, or pico-farad range.

Figure 6Different circuit symbols for different capacitor types

2.8. Digital Technology

After getting to know the most relevant hardware components, we move on to digital technology – a subfield of electrical engineering. To understand how digital technology helps us in programming, it is important to separate the definitions of the terms 'analog' and 'digital.'

An analog signal is continuous. Theoretically, there are infinite intermediate values between two values.

One example is an analog clock, where the hand does not tick or jump, but rotates continuously. In such an analog clock, the hand can theoretically take any position within its mechanical possibilities and thus show any time.

 An analog quantity can take any value within the definition range.

Fundamentals of Electrical Engineering

Example of an analog voltage curve:

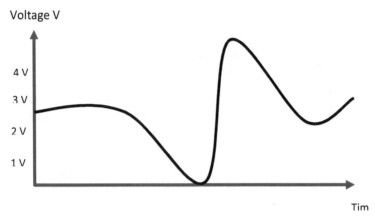

Figure 7 Analog voltage curve

This is not the case with a digital watch. Most digital watches without a dial, such as digital alarm clocks, cannot even display seconds. The clock can only show discrete values.

💡 A physical quantity, which can take only certain discrete values, is called a digital signal.

Example of a digital voltage curve:

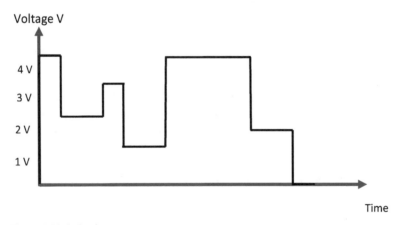

Figure 8 Digital voltage curve

14

> *Fun fact: The term 'digital' is derived from the Latin word digitus, which literally means finger. Just like our fingers, a digital signal has a countable number of values.*

Today's computing units, pocket calculators, PCs, or smartphones use only the digital system. A storage unit, a so-called bit, can either be loaded (logical "1") or not loaded (logical "0").

To be able to calculate with a physical quantity, for example the outside temperature, we need sensors that convert the heat property of the air into an electrical signal.

 A sensor converts a physical quantity into an electrical signal, in this case the temperature into an analog voltage.

This analog signal is then converted into a digital signal. Analog-to-digital converters ADC (analog-to-digital converter) are used for this.

 The conversion of an analog signal into a digital signal is called sampling.

With this digital quantity we can then perform our usual arithmetic operations (addition, subtraction, ...).

If you want to output an analog quantity afterwards, for example to operate the motor of a fan, the digital quantity must be converted back into an analog quantity.

 The conversion of a digital quantity into an analog one is called filtering. Digital-to-analog converters (DAC) are used for this purpose.

Fundamentals of Electrical Engineering

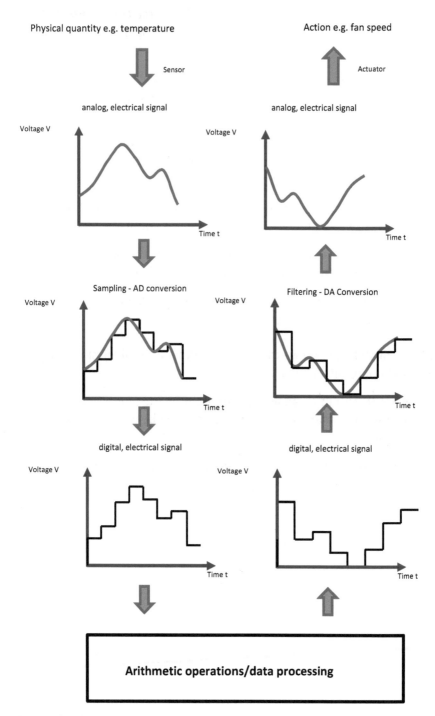

Physical quantity e.g. temperature

Sensor

analog, electrical signal

Sampling - AD conversion

digital, electrical signal

Action e.g. fan speed

Actuator

analog, electrical signal

Filtering - DA Conversion

digital, electrical signal

Arithmetic operations/data processing

Figure 9 Flowchart

Be aware that information is lost during the analog-digital conversion, because analog values are "rounded" to a digital one.

 When an analog signal is sampled, information is lost. The losses depend on how accurately the signal is digitized.

Depending on the application, it is not important whether the digital value is rounded to whole °C, i. e. 19 °C, instead of 19.5 °C.

With pictures, videos or audio files, however, the situation is quite different. Due to the digitalization during recording, information and thus data quality is lost. It should be said, however, that these effects are hardly noticeable thanks to state-of-the-art technology. The scanning is way more subtle than our perception thresholds.

2.8.1. Number Systems of a Microcontroller

This chapter is dedicated to number systems to explain how the microcontroller interprets numbers.
We all know the decimal system from our everyday life. The fact that we use ten digits is simply because we have ten fingers and the Arabic numerical system was built on this basis.

We count from zero to nine. Then we need an additional digit to represent the next higher number.
After the ones come the tens, hundreds, thousands and so on. To be able to represent this, we write the numbers one after the other. The further to the front of the complete number it is, we assign a higher value to a number.

Mathematics does not know this interpretation. It calculates with powers. Number 10 forms the basis. The location of the number corresponds to the power.
The tens correspond to 10^1, the hundreds to 10^2, the thousands to 10^3, etc.
Subconsciously, we have been applying this rule all our lives. For example, we interpret the number 1273 as 1000 + 200 + 70 + 3.
Every number can be decomposed into digits multiplied by a power of ten.
$$1273 = 1000 + 200 + 70 + 3 = 1 \cdot 10^3 + 2 \cdot 10^2 + 7 \cdot 10^1 + 3 \cdot 10^0$$

Fundamentals of Electrical Engineering

But what if we do not take 10 as the basis for our number-system, but 2? Then we would have a binary system, because there are not ten numbers, but only two, namely 0 and 1.

How can we represent the number 2 in this system? The same way we represent the number 10 in the decimal system: with an additional digit. The number two is thus represented as "10".

Then the locations do not define the weighting anymore, $10^0, 10^1, 10^2, ...$ but $2^0, 2^1, 2^2, ...$

The number 1001, for example, is interpreted in the binary system as

$1001 = 1 \cdot 2^3 + 0 \cdot 2^2 + 1 \cdot 2^1 + 1 \cdot 2^0 = 1 \cdot 8 + 0 \cdot 4 + 1 \cdot 2 + 1 \cdot 1$
In the decimal system, the binary 1011 thus corresponds to 11.

The following table shows the representation of numbers in the binary system.

Display in decimal system	Representation in binary system
0	0
1	1
2	10
3	11
4	100
5	101
6	110
7	111
8	1000
9	1001
10	1010
11	1011
12	1100
...	....
16	10000
32	100000
128	10000000
256	100000000
512	1000000000

Now you get the joke: There are only "10" kinds of people. Those who understand binary code and those who do not.

One digit is often called a bit. A bit can only assume the state "1" or "0". A byte is eight bits, therefore a byte can take the value range of 0000000 (decimal zero) or 11111111 (decimal 255). This will be of great importance later on, for example with the data types of variables.
If you want to pass a number to a microcontroller as a binary number, you mark this by writing a B in front of the number.
B1011

Why is the binary system so important for us? It is because the computer has no fingers, but only knows the states "voltage" or "no voltage". All variables, operations, functions, etc. are stored on the lowest level as bits and bytes.

There are other number systems, for example the octal system with the base eight (marked with o in front of the number, e. g. o127) or the hexadecimal system with the base 16 (marked with ox in front of the number, e. g. oxE3). For our purposes, it is sufficient to understand the binary system.

3. The Arduino Platform Explained

After having summarized the most important electrical engineering basics and understood that a microcontroller works with digital values, the following chapter explains what Arduino is exactly, where the name comes from and what different versions are available.

3.1. What Is Arduino Anyway?

Arduino describes a physical computing platform. This entails the creation of an interactive system through the use and interaction of hardware and software. This system reacts to events in the real world by recording these analog values through sensors.

This enables even laymen to implement complex projects quickly. Hobbyists, inventors and tinkerers from all over the world use the Arduino platform. Many companies, such as 3D printer manufacturers, also occasionally use components that are compatible with the Arduino platform. In the meantime, many students are learning to appreciate the system and consider the platform an easy-to-use introduction to microprocessors.

In common parlance, the term Arduino stands for the boards, i. e. boards including microcontrollers and peripherals, as well as for software and programming.

3.1.1. Origin

The founders of the Arduino platform, Massimo Banzi and David Cuartielles, wanted to provide access to microcontroller programming to as many people as possible.

Therefore, the platform's accessibility for people without in-depth technical knowledge is of great importance. For example, the structure of the programming is slightly modified. Complex libraries are written by trained programmers and the end user can easily use them without understanding the full scope of the library.

Fun fact: Arduino was the name of the bar where the founders met to promote their idea. This is how the name of a small coffee shop in an Italian province became a world-famous brand with a huge community.

Furthermore, both the hardware and the software are open source. This means that all features are freely accessible.

For example, you can download the schematics and layouts of the Arduino boards free of charge from the official Arduino homepage. On the other hand, this makes it very easy to reproduce the technology and many Chinese companies have started to do so.

3.1.2. Hardware – The Arduino Board

Because the technology is accessible to everyone, the Arduino platform has quickly gained popularity. Large communities have formed and technology companies are producing sensors and actuators that are precisely tailored to the Arduino ecosystem.

Figure 10 Atmel chip series

The hardware usually consists of a microcontroller with ambient circuitry (peripherals). The built-in microcontroller is part of the Atmel-megaAVR series, which is an 8-bit microcontroller family produced by the chip manufacturer Microship from the USA. The AVR family was chosen because of its easy programmability, in the version with standard DIP chip package.

The official name Arduino is protected, which is why replicas often have a similar name, but may only be advertised as "Arduino-compatible". Examples of replicas of the Arduino Uno are the Elegoo Uno, the Funduino Uno or the "Sunfounder Board for Arduino Uno".

The equipment of the different boards is more or less extensive, depending on the model. The various Arduino models are presented below. We start with the largest, most extensive model, the Arduino MEGA 2560 R3, and break it down step by step until we arrive only at nothing but a chip without peripherals, the Atthiny.

3.2.   The Arduino Family at a Glance

3.2.1.   Arduino Mega 2560

The largest Arduino is the Arduino Mega 2560. Its name is derived from the microcontroller used, which is an ATmega2560 built-in.

The chip has 54 digital and 16 analog or other important pins, such as GND pins and pins for buses. The Arduino has a USB-B connector, which allows it to be connected to a PC and programmed. It can be powered via a USB port or via an external power supply. For more information, see the chapter "five ways to power the Arduino".

 Because of its large internal memory and many inputs and outputs, the Arduino Mega 2560 is designed for large projects.

Today, many 3D printers are based on an ATmega2560 chip.

With a suitable shield (see chapter 3.5), even an ordinary Mega 2560 can become the mainboard of a 3D printer. The Marlin software is also freely accessible.

3.2.2. Arduino Uno

The model in the middle of the Arduino family is the Arduino Uno.

It comes on a circuit board with soldered socket strips. All important pins like analog and digital in- and outputs are available, as well as different buses to control e. g. an SD card.

Compared to the Arduino MEGA 2560, there are significantly fewer pins. However, in most cases not all Arduino Uno pins are needed.

Furthermore, the Arduino Uno costs only slightly more than half the price of an Arduino Mega. Thanks to its high popularity, it has a large community with a lot of matching accessories and extensions.

 The Arduino Uno can be described as the all-rounder in the Arduino family. It is ideally suited for beginners. Therefore, this model is used for the projects in this book.

3.2.3. Arduino Nano

The Arduino Nano differs strongly from its bigger brothers and sisters. The USB-B plug is replaced by a mini-USB plug. Furthermore, the connector socket for an external power supply has also been removed, which is also its greatest strength. It uses the same microcontroller as the Arduino Uno, but requires only a quarter of the board area.

 The Arduino Nano is ideal for projects where saving space is important, but you do not want to compromise on functionality.

3.2.4. Arduino Pro Mini

If you are looking for an even smaller option, the Arduino Pro Mini might be the right choice for you. In contrast to the Arduino Nano, the Arduino Pro Mini does not have a USB port, so that area of the board can be removed. An external adapter is therefore required for programming.

3.2.5. ATthiny

The ATthiny family is not directly connected to the Arduino family. Since the controllers can be programmed via the Arduino IDE, they are mentioned here to illustrate how minimalistically an Arduino project can be built.

The ATthiny chips are "naked" microcontrollers without peripherals. For the use of these chips, a special board has to be developed.

An Arduino Uno can be used for programming. With its help, the ATthiny can be programmed.

In addition to the designs presented, there are also various modifications and special cases for one area of application.

 Since the structure of Arduino is open source, there are many copies available from manufacturers in the Far East. These usually contain much cheaper hardware components, which increases the probability of failure.

After getting to know the features of the different versions, we will now have a look at the circuit board layout of an Arduino. The following chapter will focus on the Arduino Uno, since it is the standard model. It offers a mixture of connectivity and ease of use for beginners.

3.3. Construction of the Arduino Uno

The board is equipped with many components around the microcontroller, such as the power supply and USB ports for programming via PC communication.

Figure 11 Arduino UNO seen from above

3.3.1. Connections and Interfaces

Let us start with the most obvious aspects: the pins and the sockets.

USB socket: The USB type B socket can be used for power supply and communication with a computer. For power supply, make sure that the external USB port provides sufficient power.

 The low voltage socket is used only for power supply. It has an input voltage range of 7 - 12 V DC. DC stands for direct current.

Again, make sure you use a power supply with sufficient power.

In the upper and lower areas are two rows of beech trees with pins for digital use. The pins TX and RX are connectors for a serial bus connection. The digital pins 2 - 13 can be used for input or output. The pins can either have the value 0 V or 5 V. Intermediate stages are not compatible. The tilde next to the pins means that these pins can be used as a PWM signal, for example to drive a motor. These pins can also be used to generate a voltage between 0 V and 5 V.

27

Next to it is a ground pin (GND), a pin for an analog reference voltage (AREF), and two I2C pins (SCL and SDA) for an I²C bus connection. There is also a reset button, which is useful if you want to reset the microcontroller without disconnecting it from the power source.

The analog pins A0 - A5 can be found in the lower area. These can also be used as inputs and take values from **0 V to 5 V** including intermediate stages.

 How can the Arduino calculate with an analog voltage? What components are required?

Solution: The analog voltage at the pin is first digitized by means of an AD converter. The Arduino has an integrated 10Bit-AD-converter for this purpose.

Most pins, whether digital or analog, are routed directly to the microcontroller, which takes us straight to the heart of the device, the AT-MEGA328P.

The ARMEGA328P forms the brain of the Arduino. The chip is available in two versions, in the plug-on-and-plug-off version with a socket on the board and in the flat SMD (surface mounted device) version. Although optically different, it is the same chip with the same characteristics and connection possibilities.

Figure 12 Arduino UNO with pluggable chip

Figure 13 Arduino UNO with fixed SMD chip

In addition to the main chip, another chip is installed, the ATMEGA16U2. This chip is mounted directly next to the USB socket. It converts the USB signals into serial signals which the ATMEGA328P can understand. It serves as a 'translator' between PC and ATMEGA328P.

Two LEDs are attached to the data lines Tx and Rx. If they flicker, they indicate a functioning serial connection. This will happen in several cases, for example when the microcontroller receives programming or program data from the PC.

Besides these LEDs there is another diode indicating the operating voltage (labelled ON) and a LED (L) connected to digital pin 13. This can be used, for example, to check whether the program is controlling this pin while executing a program.

 Pins that are found on the board multiple times are directly connected to each other. This includes, for example, the GND pins or the pins to the data interfaces (SDA, SCL).

The remaining components, such as two large capacitors and resistors, are used for voltage stabilization or as protective circuits. The oval 16 MHz quartz clocks the microcontroller.

Finally, there is a component that is responsible for the power supply. It converts the input voltage, which lies within the range of 7 - 12 V, into a constant 5 V DC voltage for the microcontroller and 3.3 V for external applications. However, there is something to be considered here, otherwise the voltage converter or an external device may break down with a plume of smoke.

As already mentioned, the input voltage of the low voltage socket is fed to the voltage regulator. Alternatively, the voltage can be fed directly via the vin-pin.

The Vin-Pin is connected to the low voltage socket.

 Many adapters or extensions are designed for 5 V or 3.3 V. Therefore, you may only connect them to the vin-pin if you use a 5 V power supply or the power supply via USB. Otherwise you must select the 5 V pin.

Before you plug a power supply into the Arduino, always check if there are extensions connected to the vin-pin.

Furthermore, it should be noted that the 5 V voltage converter is only designed for very low currents. According to the data sheet, it can deliver a maximum of 200 mA, i. e. 1 W power. When operating several motors, for example, an external power supply must always be connected, otherwise the voltage regulator will be overloaded.

3.3.2. Pinout

The pinout diagram is important for correctly addressing the pins later in the program. Each pin has one or more labels.

The names of the pins are also written on the side of the Arduino. Sometimes you may want to program when the Arduino is out of range. It might thus be helpful to set a bookmark on this particular page.

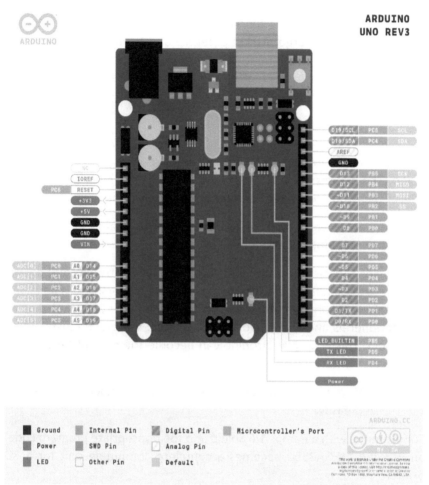

Figure 14 Pinout of the Arduino UNO

The analog pins A0 - A5 can also be used as digital pins D14 - D19 if required.

3.4. Other Hardware

The Arduino platform has quickly gained popularity. Many companies have identified the large market potential and have focused on extensions and suitable components for the Arduino platform. Some of the most important sensors, actuators and boards are presented below.

3.5. Arduino Shields

Arduino Shields are expansion boards that are the same size of an Arduino. The dimensions and pin assignments are designed to match the pins of the Arduino and can be placed directly onto the Arduino.

 Arduino Shields are custom-fit expansion boards, which are developed for a special one.

The shields themselves often contain additional electronic components that are intended for a specific application. The Motorshield is an example of this. It fits on an Arduino Uno and Arduino MEGA2560. Motor drivers, peripherals and sockets for connecting DC motors are installed on the shield. This is how an Arduino can become the control center for a model car.

 With the help of these shields, even larger projects can be realized easily.

For example, with a Ramps 1.6 Shield and the appropriate program code, an Arduino MEGA2560 becomes a complete computing unit for a 3D printer.

In connection with such shields, sensors and/or actuators are usually required.

3.6. Sensors and Actuators

In chapter 2.8, Digital Technology, we have learned that sensors generate an electrical, mostly analog signal from a physical quantity.

Alternatively, sensors with integrated evaluation electronics are also available, which can measure the physical quantity and transmit the measurement results to the Arduino via an interface. The interface can be one (or more) data cable. All available sensors have both advantages and disadvantages. Depending on the type of sensor, you have to inter-rogate the sensor differently to retrieve the desired data. Since sensors are a big part of the Arduino ecosystem, we will learn how to control them later on by looking at five sensors.

The term actuator is less common than sensor.

Actuators are the counterpart of sensors. They convert an electrical sig-nal as a change of a physical quantity. For example, an electric motor con-verts the output signal into mechanical motion, or a heating element con-verts the output signal into heat.

3.7. Breadboard and (Jumper) Cable

In order to build a circuit quickly, we need a so-called breadboard.

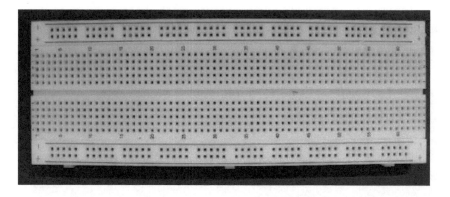

Figure 15 Plug-in board

A breadboard consists of many rows and columns, whereby the inner rows are connected to each other and the power supply is applied on the outside. The following figure shows which contacts of the bread-board are connected to each other.

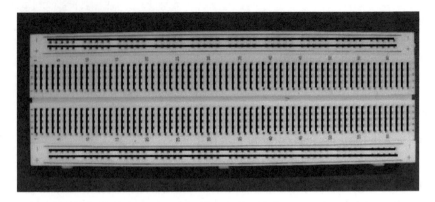

Figure 16 Plug-in board with marked connections

Pegboards are available in many sizes and designs. The connections are almost always identical. Every Arduino beginner's set includes such a breadboard, usually in combination with jumper cables.

Instead of soldering cables together, we use jumper cables and connectors. Jumper cables have a pin at their end that fits into the sockets of the Arduino and the connector board.

Figure 17 Jumper cable

Connectors, on the other hand, are only designed to make connections on the breadboard.

Figure 18 Connectors

Due to the simple plug-in mechanism, circuits can be set up quickly. Nevertheless, you always have to pay attention to which rows are connected!

For beginners in the Arduino range, so-called starter kits are recommended. These are offered by different manufacturers in different sizes. Depending on their size, they contain LEDs, sensors, motors, displays and many other components. A breadboard and cables are part of the basic equipment.

4. Programming Basics

In the following, the basics of C programming are explained. It is, of course, impossible to give a complete, comprehensive introduction within the scope of one chapter. Thus, the aim of this section is merely to explain the logic and structure of a C program in the context of Arduino programming. For further information on C programming, I recommend "C. Programming from the beginning" by Helmut Erlenkötter.

To breathe life into a microcontroller, the empty memory cells of the microcontroller have to be filled with meaningful code. This applies not only to the Arduino family, but to any chip-based electronic system. A memory cell is called a bit. The cell can either be filled, represented by a "1", or it can be empty, represented by a "0". Also known is the unit byte, which corresponds to 8 bits.
These still empty bits and bytes are filled by programming. For this purpose, a code must be created.

At this point, a program (source code) is nothing more than a multiline text.

 A program code can be opened and edited in any ordinary text editor. You do not need an exotic program to do this.

This text is then interpreted by a compiler. It translates the program code into so-called machine code. This code is then transmitted to the microcontroller.

To create the code, you need a suitable programming language that the compiler understands.
Each programming language uses its own syntax, punctuation and signal words. If you use a different programming language than the one intended, the compiler cannot "understand"/interpret the code.

The microcontroller, which is used on an Arduino, can be programmed via its own user interface (Arduino IDE). Variants of the programming language C, C++, as well as Java can be used.

The fact that Java can be used is of particular advantage for programmers who have already worked on graphical user interfaces with Java. Java was previously often used for web applications.

For the most part, however, Arduinos are programmed in C, occasionally in C++. Nearly every tutorial, manual and reference book about Arduino is based on the programming language C.
Programming with C is almost unlimited. It is beginner-friendly and easy to understand.
In the following, the essential topics for Arduino programming are presented.

 All the following information refers to programming the Arduino with C. This is mostly general information about C programming, but there are small peculiarities typical to Arduino.

4.1. Comments and Instructions

4.1.1. Comments

Comments on the clarity and structure of a program. A comment is not translated by the compiler. It serves only the human being to understand the program better.

Comments are indicated with two slashes.

// this is a comment

If you want to comment out several lines at once, start with a slash followed by a star. You can also close the comment section with an asterisk followed by a slash.

/* this is a comment

this here is still a comment

*this is also a comment */*

When several people are working on a project together or several people are supposed to understand the same code, comments are essential.

Furthermore, it is recommended to add a header comment at the beginning of a program, which contains all important data about the program. For example:

/ Program code: Example Arduino Project*

Author: Max Mustermann

Created: 12.12.2021

Project status: 01.01.2022

/

4.1.2. Instructions

Statements (eng. instructions) are the core of a program. They can be arithmetic operations or input and output instructions. Defining variables, calling functions or aborting a loop are further examples of an instruction.

A statement ends with a semicolon. This is how the compiler knows that the previous should be interpreted as an instruction.

Instruction1; //Comment on Instruction1

Instruction2;

Instruction3;

4.2. Variables

Variables are numbers that can be changed during the runtime of a program. They are used to store values or numbers. Variables must be initialized at the beginning of a program and can be changed during the process. The naming of variables should be meaningful and short. For example, a variable in which a temperature value is stored could be called Temp1.

 If there are several similar variables, it is recommended to distinguish them by their names or indices.

4.2.1. Data Types

In C, there are different types of variables which differ in size (memory requirements) or content.

For example, if a variable can only become 0 or 1, a single bit of memory is enough to map the information. It therefore makes no sense to assign 2, 3 or 10 bits to the variable. It is always better to program sparingly. At the beginning, there are no problems, but with experience the projects grow and you can quickly run out of memory if you "give" each variable the maximum memory.

The variables were just a simple example. There are, of course, much more complex methods to "save" memory:

 An example of suboptimal programming is the Windows user interface. Everyone is familiar with Windows and has probably used it before. Windows was also programmed. By now, the source code of Windows is gigantic and no single person can fully grasp it in its entirety.

However, a large part of the code is not essential. Due to the complexity and volume of the code, however, not even the programmers responsible today can say for themselves whether parts of the code can be removed without affecting it elsewhere.

Following the motto "never change a running system", Windows is thus much larger than it should be, with almost 60 GB of required memory.

The following table lists the most important variable types with their value range. There are still innumerable further variable types, which are negligible for newcomers.

Name	Abbre- viation	Required storage space	Maximum value range as decimal	Special feature
Boolean	boolean	1 bit	0 and 1 (True or False)	
Byte	byte	8 Bit = 1 Byte	0...255	No negative values
Character	char	8 Bit = 1 Byte	-128...127	Saves a letter
Unsigned character	unsigned char	8 Bit = 1 Byte	0...255	No negative values
Integer	int	16 Bit = 2 Byte	32.768...32.767	Only integers
Unsigned in- tegrity	unsigned int	16 Bit = 2 Byte	0...65535	Only integers
Long	long	32 Bit = 4 Byte	-2.147.483.648 ... 2.147.483.647	
Unsigned long	unsigned long	32 Bit = 4 Byte	0 .... 4.294.967.295	No negative values
Float	float	32 Bit = 4 Byte	$-3,4028235 \cdot 10^{38} ...$ $3,4028235 \cdot 10^{38}$	(Floating) decimal numbers

 We want to measure and store the height of a child throughout its life. The height in cm is used and stored in a variable. Which data type is best for saving the size?

Solution: The data type byte would be most useful. With this data type, you can store values from 0 to 255 cm, in our example as centimeters (255 cm = 2.55 m). The datatype char would also work, but it is used to store letters and not numbers. All other datatypes like int, long or float would also work, but need much more memory.

Beside the variables, i. e. variable numbers, there are constants, too. These remain unchanged, as their name suggests.

 For a constant, we write the term const in front of the data type. It is thus obvious, especially for the reader of the program, that it represents a constant.

Alternatively, the #define-command can be used. In this case, the compiler replaces all occurrences of the specified constant (example constant) with the prescribed value (here 6).

#define example constant 6

Or

const int Example constant = 6;

For beginners, both variants are equivalent, but const is used more frequently.

4.2.2. Operators

You can calculate with variables or compare different variables. This will soon become very important, especially in the following section about functions and loops. Therefore, we will go through the most important operators together. These are known from mathematics, the peculiarities of their syntax under C are explained here briefly. It is also important to understand that the result of a comparison can be either "true" or "false". But for this we need to know the rules about when to make which decision.

Operator	Meaning	Example	Function
Arithmetic Operators			
=	Assignment	X=3;	
+	Addition	x=Y+2;	
++	Increment	x++;	X is increased by one. Short notation for x=x+1;
-	Subtraction	x=Y-2;	
--	Decree	x--;	X is increased by one. Short notation for x=x-1;
*	Multiplication	x=y*2	
/	Division	x=y/2	
%	Modulo	X= 10%3;	Delivers the rest to Division. 10 divided by 3 yields 3, remainder 1, so x takes the value 1.
Comparison Operators			
<	Smaller?	3<5	
<=	Smaller equal?	3<=5	
>	Bigger?	5>3	
>=	Greater or equal?	5>=3	
==	Now?	5==4	

!=	Unequal?	4!=5	
Logical Operators			
!	Negation	x=!y;	If y is true, x becomes false and vice versa
&&	And	x= 1&&0	true corresponds to true, zero corresponds to false, therefore x is also false (because both must be true)
||	Or	x=1||0	true is true, zero is false, therefore x is true

4.3. Functions

I am sure you have encountered functions at some point in school. y = mx+c is the classic example of a linear function. The basic idea is that you pass a number x the function and then get a number y.

 A function during programming is not limited to input or output values as numbers.

For example, you can pass a letter or a whole word to a function instead of a number. You will not necessarily get a number in return.

As "feedback" to a function, for example, a motor can rotate, a picture or a text can be displayed.

Let us use the function analogRead() as an example, which is discussed in more detail in chapter 5.3.4. The function reads the voltage value applied to an analog input pin of the Arduino.

The function is told in the form of the input parameter which pin of the Arduino is to be read out. The function returns a value which corresponds to the voltage at the corresponding pin.

Zero stands for 0 V and 1023 stands for 5 V.

Example:

int Temperature;

Temperature = analogRead(A8);

The "Temperature" variable is assigned the value applied to pin A8.

4.4. Loops and Conditions

Loops and conditions are auxiliary tools to control a program more pre-cisely and efficiently. Loops can be used to repeat certain program sec-tions and conditions can be used to skip or execute program sections un-der certain program conditions.

When it comes to programming, one of the most important statements is the if statement.

4.4.1. If Statement

The "if-then" statement is only executed if a certain condition is fulfilled. The condition is written in round brackets after the signal word "if". It is important to understand that the condition is checked for truth. See also the operator table 4.2.2.

All statements to be executed if the condition is true are written in curly brackets.

if(condition){statement1
;
statement2;

...
}

If the condition is met, the program code in the curly brackets is executed.

If the condition is not met, the if statement is skipped and the program picks back up after the curly brackets.

Programming Basics

If you want to execute alternative statements, i. e. if the uncondition is not true, use the else statement. This is optional, you can omit it.

Example:

```
int Temperature;              //      variable      for
temperature

string Status;                // Variable for the status

if(temperature>24){           // Only if the temperature is >
24°C

Status = "it is too warm";    //... it is too warm

}

else{

Status="it is not too warm";

}
```

Only when the temperature value rises above 24 is the variable status "it's too why" assigned.

If no comparison operator is used, every number not equal to zero is interpreted as "true." Only the zero itself is interpreted as "false."

 Check for yourself: When is the if condition fulfilled? When is it not?

```
if(3>5) { }

if(3<5) { }

if(3) { }......

if(0) { }......

if(!3) { }......

if(2==2) { }......

if( (4>2) && (3<1) ) { }
```

Solution:

1. No, 3 is less than 5, so the if statement is not executed.

2. Yes, 3 is less than 5, so the if statement is executed.

3. Yes, 3 is a non-zero number, so it is interpreted as "true" and the if statement is executed.

4. No, the number zero is interpreted as "wrong" and the if statement is not executed.

5. No, the number three is interpreted as true, but negated, so the if statement is not executed.

6. Correct, because 2==2 is a true result.

 Attention, here "==" must be used to check a true statement. The operator "=" is an assignment, not a check. If(2=2) would result in an error – a common error!

7. No, it must be both 4 greater than 2 and 3 less than 1, so the if statement is not executed.

4.4.2. For Statement

The for statement is a bit more complex.

The for statement repeats the statements written in curly brackets as long as the condition is true. Oftentimes, a counter variable is defined for this purpose, which is counted up or down.

Structure:

for (initialization of the counting variable; condition; increment) {

}

Example:

```
for (int i=0; i <= 10; i++){

// statement is executed 11 times in total

}
```

The instruction in this case is executed eleven times because the counting variable starts at i=0 and the check condition is i<=10. If i<10, the loop would only run ten times.

4.4.3. While Loop

A while loop runs on and on until the condition in the round brackets becomes "false." The loop can run infinitely, too, if the condition never becomes logical (boolean) "false."

A while loop runs for as long as the condition of the loop is true. If nothing is executed in the while loop that affects the condition, it runs infinitely.

Example of a loop that is executed ten times.

```
int i = 0;                    //counter variable

while(i < 10) {

    i++;                      // increase i by 1

}
```

4.4.4. Th While

The do-while loop works along the same lines as the while loop. The main difference is that the condition is checked only at the end of the loop. This means that the loop is executed at least once.

Example:

```
int i = 0;                    //counter variable

do {

    i++;                      // increase i by 1

} while(i < 10)
```

4.4.5. Loop Loop

The loop loop is an arduinotypical, endless loop. It is required so that the microcontroller always has something to do. You could think of the loop loop as the microcontroller's "sleep mode." It is just like a while-loop which is always "true."

4.5. Libraries

Libraries are another huge advantage of the open source concept Arduino. A library is basically the non-physical extension of the functional range of the Arduino software. It adds further commands and functions.

Libraries are usually built on large chunks of code, but understanding this code is not necessary in order to use them.

For example, it is very tedious to program the control of a servo motor by hand.
Instead, there is a ready-made library through which you can control the servos with simple functions. After all, why should we program the control ourselves if someone else has already made the effort?

 A library must be loaded at the start of a program. This is realized by #include.

For example, the command for using the Servo.h library
#include <Servo.h>.

 To use a library, the library file must be located in the installation folder of the Arduino IDE. If the library is installed via the Arduino IDE, this happens automatically.

In the next chapter, you will learn the easiest way to do this and how to install the Arduino IDE and the most important functions.

5. The Arduino IDE

The Arduino IDE (integrated developing environment) is a free program that, like the whole Arduino system, is designed for ease of use. The user is given a framework for his program.

 With the help of the Arduino IDE, you can program all Arduino models, be it Arduino Nano, Arduino Uno or Arduino Mega.

The installation of the Arduino IDE is almost self-explanatory.

The official Arduino website can be reached at arduino.cc. The software section provides access to the download. The software is available for Windows, Mac OS X and Linux.

Since the majority of readers use a Windows PC, the installation for Windows will be covered in the following. The installation for Mac OS X and Linus are very similar. Meanwhile, a Microsoft app is also available, which can be downloaded from the corresponding store.

Since not everyone has an account there and cannot use the store, the alternative download is shown as an exe file. Download via the ZIP folder is also possible, but a few clicks more complex.

Download the Arduino IDE

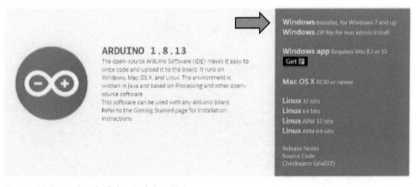

Figure 19 Download of the Arduino IDE

A donation request appears before the download. The Arduino platform is completely free of charge, which is why they depend on donations. Whether or how much you donate has no effect on the download or the program itself. Once the download has started, all you have to do is follow the instructions and install the software. This usually takes a few minutes.

5.1. Structure of an Arduino Program

Once the software is installed, you can open the Arduino IDE for the first time. A so-called sketch appears with the current date in its name. A sketch is the name of the program code.

The sketch consists of a relatively empty page, which is also the basic framework of any Arduino program.

 The two sections setup and loop are mandatory and must be present in every program.

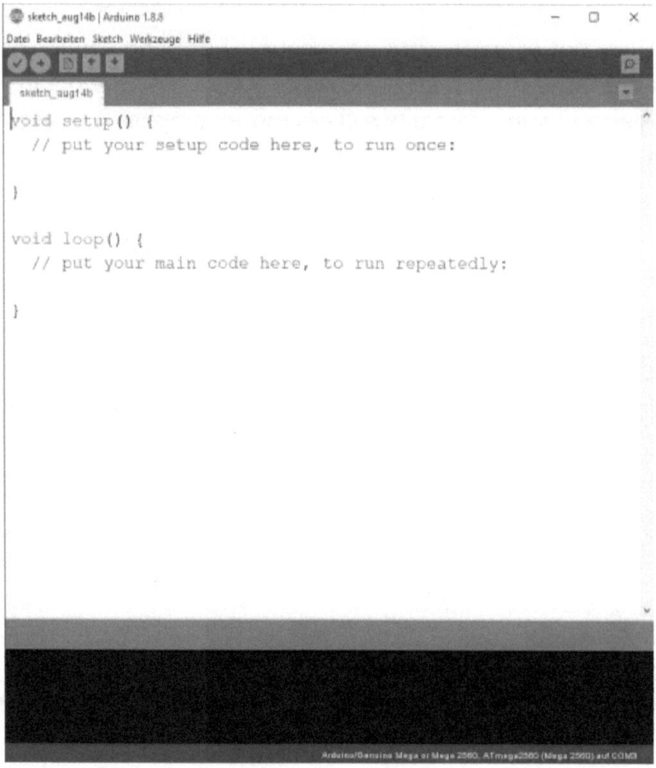

Figure 20 Arduino IDE

5.1.1. void setup(){ }

void setup(){ } represents a function that is executed once after the microcontroller has been started. It is called setup by default and can theoretically be renamed as desired. However, it is recommended not to change the name for the sake of clarity.

 In the setup() part, for example, inputs and outputs are defined or external hardware is initialized.

 Global variables or libraries must be defined or included outside of the setup(), otherwise they cannot be used in other functions.

When and how something is defined or initialized, we will discuss in detail in the first practical example (6.1Control LEDs – Traffic Light Circuit).

5.1.2. void loop(){ }

void loop(){}, on the other hand, describes a program that is executed continuously (loop). The data type void is prefixed to functions that do not return a value.

 After switching on the microcontroller, the setup function is executed once. Then the loop function is executed and repeated indefinitely.

The loop function contains the actual program sequence, whether a LED is flashing, sensors are read in or a motor is to be moved.

5.1.3. Add Libraries

We already know what libraries are and why they are useful. But what is the easiest way to add them?

In the Arduino IDE, there is an overview of all libraries, similar to an app store you can search and install different libraries there, all for free, of course. To do this, go to Sketch, then scroll down to include libraries. A menu with all available libraries will open. Click on Manage libraries to open an overview where you can update your current libraries. You can also search for various libraries and add them via Install.

If you download a library as a zip file, it can be installed alternatively via Sketch > Include Library > Include Zip Library.

You can then include the libraries via Sketch > Include Library and select the library to include. Alternatively, you can also include the library manually with the #include command at the start of a program.

5.2. Indent

One of the most important tools to make the program code easy to understand is indentation. This allows program parts to be structured and visually separated. Paragraphs can also be used for clarity at the beginning, but for larger projects it is recommended to avoid long paragraphs.

```
int x = 1
void loop() {
   if (x == 1) {
      for (i = 0; i < 10; i++) {
         Serial.println(x);
      }
   }
}
```

A rule for indenting is to indent every new program layer.

 A new programming level begins after curly brackets, for example, for a function, a loop or a statement.

The advantage is that the closing curly bracket '}' is directly under the statement or loop to which it belongs. The following figure shows the different programming levels. You can immediately see which lines of code belong to the if statement and which to the for loop.

```
int x = 1
void loop() {
  if (x == 1) {
    for (i = 0; i < 10; i++) {
      Serial.println(x);
    }
  }
}
```

There is another advantage: If you mark a curly bracket with the mouse, the corresponding bracket appears on a red background. This way, you can quickly check whether you have forgotten a bracket or have too many.

The Arduino IDE has an auto formatting function. With CTRL+T, the code is automatically formatted.

5.3. Important Functions

As you can probably imagine, there are now almost infinitely many projects, libraries and functions. New ones are added every day.

Accordingly, it is virtually impossible to explain all functions in their entirety. The description of some libraries and functions is more comprehensive than this complete beginner's guide.

Therefore, we concentrate only on the most important functions that are found in almost every program, for example the function to read in and evaluate external signals.

Let us start with the most important ones.

5.3.1. Delay and Delaymicroseconds

The processor processes the commands at breakneck speed. Often, however, you will want the processor to pause for a short time at one point in the program.

The function delay() is responsible for this.

You enter the desired waiting time in milliseconds into the function. 1000 milliseconds correspond to one second. If we want the program to wait two seconds at one position, we write

delay(2000);

delaymicroseconds() is used if we want to wait less than one millisecond. In this case, we enter the time in microseconds. 1000 microseconds correspond to one millisecond. If we want to wait for 200 microseconds, we write

delaymicroseconds(200);

5.3.2. analogRead()

The analogRead() function reads the value of an analog pin. The value is returned to the function.

For example, if we want to know the voltage value at pin A5, we write

analogRead(A5);

To save the value, we have to write it into a variable afterwards.

Since the Arduino only calculates digitally, this value, which is in the range between 0 V to 5 V, will be converted into a number.

 The Arduino boards contain a 10-bit analog-to-digital converter. The AD converter assigns an integer value between 0 and 1023 to the input voltages on the analog pins, which are between 0 V and 5 V.

In an Arduino Uno, a so-called quantization stage corresponds to $\frac{5V}{1024} = 0{,}0049\,V = 4{,}9\,mV$

If you want to use the voltage value at a pin directly as a value in the program, the conversion is

Voltage in V = analogRead(analog pin) · 0,0049;

 The function analogRead(); returns an integer value. If the value is to be stored in a variable of a different type, a type conversion must first be performed.

5.3.3. map()

The map function is often used in combination with the analogRead() function.

The function maps one range of numbers to another. It is therefore perfectly suited to convert the value you extract from the function analogRead() into your desired range of values.

For the function to be able to execute this, the value must be converted to the lower and upper limits of the current value range and the lower and upper limits of the new value range.

For example, a measured value at analog pin A2 is to be converted into a voltage of 0 V to 5000 mV.

int measured value = analogRead(A2); // this value is 0...1023

int Voltage_in_mV = map(measured value,0,1023,0,5000);

Measured value	-> Value to be assigned.
0	-> The lower limit of the current value range
1023	-> The upper limit of the current value range.
0	-> The lower limit of the new value range.
5000	-> The upper limit of the new value range.

The value is changed from the old value range 0...1023 to the new value range 0.... 5000.

The value 141 is converted to the value 688.47

 $(\frac{141}{1024} \cdot 5000 = 688,47)$

5.3.4. analogWrite – PWM control

Similar to how the function analogRead() reads analog values, the function analogWrite() can be used to output an analog value. The digital pins, which are PWM capable, come in handy here. In the Arduino Uno these are the pins 3,5,6,9,10 and 11.

Digression PWM modulation:

If you have paid attention, you may have noticed that the analog-Write function uses digital pins for output.

How is it possible that a digital pin that can only switch 0 V or 5 V suddenly also outputs intermediate values such as 1 V, 3 V or 4.36 V?

The solution has already been mentioned and is called Pulse Width Modulation, short PWM. The German translation is not uniform; pulse duration modulation, pulse length modulation, pulse width modulation or also pulse width modulation are used, but all terms mean the same technique.

Pulse modulation describes the simulation of a certain voltage (below 5 V) by fast switching of a higher voltage (5 V) followed by voltage-free pauses. The Arduino switches the digital output on and off up to 1000 times per second. The higher the output voltage, the longer the switch-on time in which the 5 V is applied.

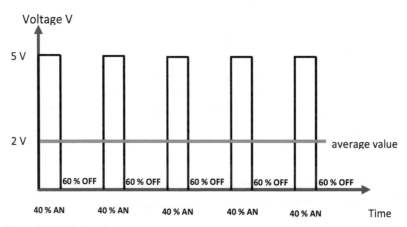

Figure 21 PWM signal

If, for example, an LED is to be operated at 2 V, only 5 V is present 40 % of the time ($\frac{2V}{5V} \cdot 100\%$). The other 60 % of the time, 0 V is applied. This results in an average of 2 V. Since the LED is switched on and off 1000 times per second, our eye does not perceive flickering, but a lower brightness. The same principle works, for example, for the speed control of a DC motor.

As users, we actually do not notice anything about the pulse width modulation. The voltage at the output is almost constantly 2 V, unless measured with a very fast measuring device, for example an oscilloscope.

The function analogWrite() has similar properties to analogRead(), but it does not return a value, after all nothing is read.

Again, the number of the corresponding PWM pin is first passed to the function. Furthermore, a value between 0 and 1023 must be passed. This corresponds to the voltage.

 If we want to output an analog voltage of 3 V at the digital PWM pin 9, we must first convert 3 V into the corresponding integer.

$$value = \frac{3V}{5V} \cdot 1023 \approx 614$$

The command would therefore be

```
analogWrite(9,614);
```

The pin designations can be found in Chapter 3.3.1 Pinout.

5.3.5. digitalRead

digitalRead() reads the value at a digital pin. To do this, the function must be informed that the pin is used as input.

As return value we get either HIGH or a one, if 5 V are applied, and LOW or zero, if no voltage is applied.

If we want to know whether pin 9 (digital pin) is HIGH or LOW, we write

```
int value;

pinMode(9,INPUT);

value = digitalRead(9);
```

5.3.6. digitalWrite

The digitalWrite() function also requires the pin to be declared as output (OUTPUT) first. The pin can then be passed to the function. Furthermore, the function must know whether the output should be HIGH or LOW.

```
pinMode(9,OUTPUT);

digitalWrite(9,LOW);
```

5.3.7. Serial.print

The Serial.print() function allows you to communicate with the Arduino via PC or to read the communication.

For this purpose, you pass a value to the function. This value can be a number, a letter, a word or something similar. The function then transmits the content to the serial interface (USB).

If you have a USB cable connected to the computer, you can read the communication in the Arduino IDE. To do this, open Tools > Serial Monitor. This is where you can see what is happening on the serial port, for example, when the Arduino is communicating with another device.

 To use the serial interface, you first have to open it. You can do this in the setup() part with the function Serial.begin(9600).

The number 9600 specifies the bitrate at which Arduino and PC communicate.

The Serial.print() function is still very useful for displaying words or data in the program. In conjunction with the Serial.print() function, you can output data and, for example, check whether the correct values are used.

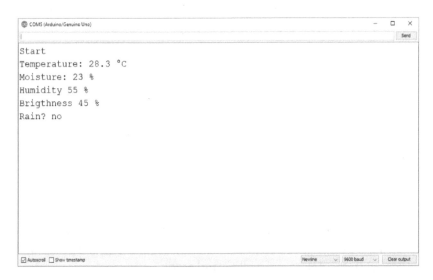

The function Serial.println() is also used often. This function adds a line break at the end of its execution in the output window (of the serial monitor), which is mainly used for clarity.

An overview of the mentioned functions and many more can be found on the official Arduino website at

https://www.arduino.cc/reference/

There, all important functions, arithmetic operations etc. are explained again.

6. Your First Projects

6.1. Control LEDs – Traffic Light Circuit

By this point, we have built a broad theoretical foundation. You are now ready to build and understand your first project from scratch. You might not have internalized everything yet, but putting your knowledge into practice will help you with that. It is not a bad thing if something does not work right away – we are simply "learning by doing."

As a first project, we will build and program a miniature version of a pedestrian traffic light circuit, a so-called demand traffic light. The structure consists of two traffic lights. First, there is a pedestrian light with the colors red and green, as well as a push button to request a green phase and a car light with the colors red, yellow and green.

By default, the traffic light is green for drivers. If the button of the pedestrian traffic light is pressed, the traffic light switches to yellow and then to red.

Afterwards, the pedestrian light will turn green and remain in this state for a few seconds. Then the light signals are switched in reverse: The pedestrian light switches to red, the car light to yellow and then to green.

6.1.1. Required Hardware

To plan our first setup, we need some components besides the Arduino.

For this project, the supply voltage for the Arduino via the USB cable is completely sufficient. A powerbank or block battery would also be a possibility.

Next, of course, we need an Arduino. As already mentioned, we use an Arduino Uno because it has enough connectors, is easy to power and has prepared pin headers. We also need the different LEDs and some cables.

For the LEDs, we use 5 mm LEDs with a forward voltage of 3 - 3.4 V at a current of 10 mA. We will also need a series resistor.

 How large must the series resistance of the LEDs be?

Solution: We can easily calculate the series resistances of the LEDs. In our example, a maximum of 2 V (5 V supply voltage minus 3 V forward voltage) should drop and about 10 mA should flow through the resistor. This results in a resistance value of

$$\frac{2V}{10\ mA} = 200\ \Omega$$

With some safety distance, we use 220 Ω. With this, we have enough buffer and the brightness is hardly noticeable.

 ! Depending on the LEDs used, the series resistor itself must be calculated.

The following table shows the hardware used for this project:

Purpose	Component
microcontroller	Arduino Uno REV 3
Power supply	USB cable
2 x Red light	5 mm LED red
2 x green light	5 mm LED green
1 x Yellow light	5 mm LED Yellow
Push button	4 pin buttons
LED series resistor	220 Ω
Pull-down resistor	10 kΩ

Instead of individual LEDs, there are also ready-made traffic light modules. These consist of the same LEDs soldered onto a board and with their connections already in place.

To operate the traffic light system, we use a push button with a total of four pins. This push button is inexpensive and is included in many starter kits.

When the button is pressed, it connects diagonally to opposite contacts. Therefore, one of these contacts is connected to 5 V and the opposite contact to the digital input pin 2 of the Arduino. When the button is pressed, 5 V is applied to pin two, corresponding to a logical HIGH.

We also need a so-called pull-down resistor.

Excursus: Pull-up and pull-down resistors:

 When using digital signals, the terms pull-up and pull-down resistor are often used. Both are high-impedance resistors (usually 4.7 kΩ or 10 kΩ).

The purpose of such a resistor is to ensure that a defined signal is always present at the digital pin. In our example, this means that if the button is not pressed, we want 0 V to be applied to the digital pin. But there is no connection to GND. The digital pin is not automatically set to 0 V, but "hangs in the air."

Therefore, we connect a resistor between GND and the pin. Since no current flows into an input pin, no voltage drops at the resistor. Therefore 0 V is also present at the pin. It is read in as logical 0. If the button is closed, the resistor prevents a connection from 5 V to 0 V.

 With a pull-up resistor, the resistance lies between the digital pin and the supply voltage. In the case of a pull-down resistor, the resistance lies between the digital pin and the ground (GND).

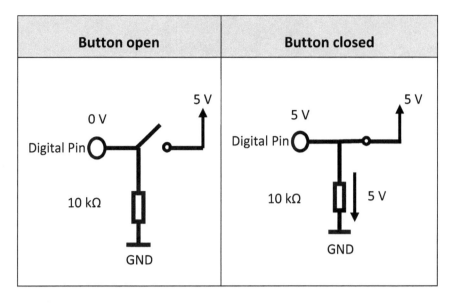

Button open	Button closed

6.1.2. Circuit Diagram

The next step is the hardware setup of the project. The following figure shows how to connect the different components.

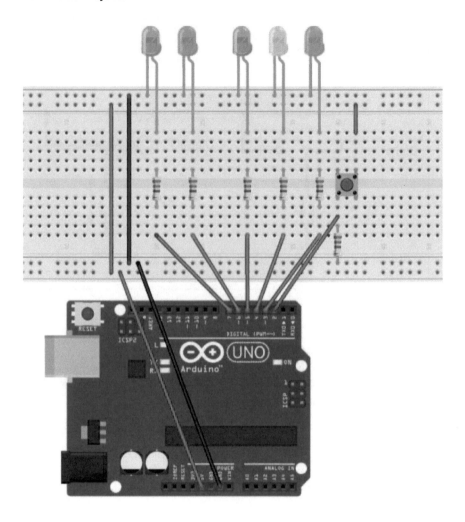

Figure 22 Circuit diagram

 We use the 5 V output of the Arduino as a power supply for the LEDs and not the vin-pin. This pin is connected to a 9 V battery voltage. If we connect it, we have to calculate a stronger series resistor for the LEDs, otherwise the LEDs would burn out.

After we have selected the hardware and set up the circuit diagram, we build the circuit on a breadboard.

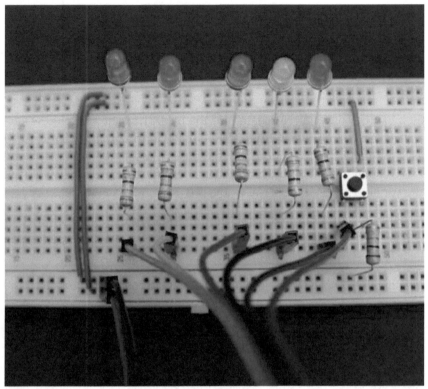

Figure 23 Assembly on the pin board

The cables lead directly to the inputs and outputs of the Arduino.

6.1.3. Programming

Finally, we take care of the programming. To start off, we connect the Arduino to the PC and start the Arduino IDE. The code for the pedestrian lights is relatively simple. The head with author and date was omitted for simplicity.

```
//////Pedestrian traffic light circuit V1.0////////

int idletime = 1000 ; // Time between changeover operations

int greenphase = 3000; // Green phase pedestrian

const int PIN_redF = 7; // Pin of red pedestrian LED

const int PIN_greenF = 6; // Pin of green pedestrian LED
```

```
const int PIN_redC = 5; // Pin of red car LED

const int PIN_yellowC = 4;

const int PIN_greenC = 3;

const int PIN_switch = 2;
```

First of all, constants are created for the pins. This is not absolutely necessary. We can always write the pin directly in the program later. However, defining constants once makes sense because, for example, if you make changes, you only have to change one value and not every value of the variable or constant in the whole program

There is an empty time. This is the time that passes between a color change. There is also a green phase, i. e. the time when the pedestrian light is green.

The idle time in the example is one second, and the green phase is three seconds.

```
void setup()

{

 pinMode( PIN_redF, OUTPUT );  //Define as inputs and outputs

 pinMode( PIN_greenF , OUTPUT);

 pinMode( PIN_redC , OUTPUT);

 pinMode( PIN_yellowC , OUTPUT);

 pinMode( PIN_greenC , OUTPUT);

 pinMode( PIN_switch , INPUT);

 //Start state pedestrian traffic light red - car traffic light green

 digitalWrite( PIN_redF, HIGH );

 digitalWrite( PIN_greenF, LOW );

 digitalWrite( PIN_redC, LOW );

 digitalWrite( PIN_yellowC, LOW );

 digitalWrite( PIN_greenC, HIGH );

}
```

Your First Projects

After the constants have been set, the setup part is executed; the start states are also set. In our example, we want the car light to be green and the pedestrian light to be red.

```
void loop() {

 if (digitalRead(PIN_switch) ) {        // only when switch is pressed

  delay(idletime); // wait one second

  digitalWrite( PIN_greenC, LOW );

  digitalWrite( PIN_yellowC, HIGH );

  delay(idletime);

  digitalWrite( PIN_yellowC, LOW );

  digitalWrite( PIN_redC, HIGH );

  delay(idletime);

  digitalWrite( PIN_redF, LOW );

  digitalWrite( PIN_greenF, HIGH );

  delay(greenphase);

  digitalWrite( PIN_greenF, LOW);

  digitalWrite( PIN_redF, HIGH);

  delay(idletime);

  digitalWrite( PIN_yellowC, HIGH );

  delay(idletime);

  digitalWrite( PIN_redC, LOW );

  digitalWrite( PIN_yellowC, LOW );

  digitalWrite( PIN_greenC, HIGH );

 }

}
```

The loop function checks whether the switch is pressed.

If this is the case, the condition if (digitalRead(PIN_switch)) is true and the if statement in curly brackets is executed.

In this mode, the car traffic light is first set to yellow and then to red after one second. Next, the pedestrian traffic light is switched to green. After the green phase, the pedestrian light switches back to red and the car light first to yellow and then back to green. It is recommended to follow the instructions step by step.

6.1.4. Upload the Code

After you have written the program, you will have to upload the code into the Arduino's memory. To do this, the Arduino is connected to the computer or laptop using the USB cable. The Arduino is recognized and any missing drivers are automatically installed. With some replicas from the Far East, it may be necessary to install special drivers.

After the Arduino is plugged in, select

Tools -> Board -> "Arduino/Genuino Uno"

Tools -> Port -> "COM5 (Arduino/Genuino Uno)"

The number of the COM port can differ and depends, for example, on how many other devices are connected to the computer.

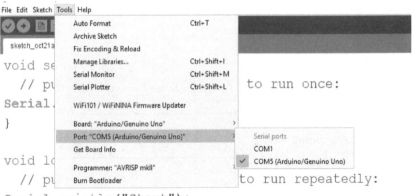

Figure 24 Selecting the COM port

After selecting the correct board and port, the program can be uploaded using the arrow.

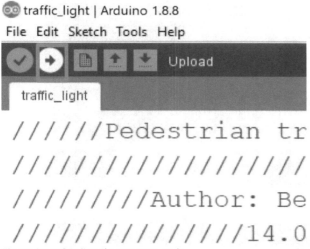

Figure 25 Uploading the program code

Finally, you will receive a summary of how much memory is needed for the program. Our small example needs only 4 % of the available memory. After the program has been uploaded to the Arduino, the green traffic light LED and the red pedestrian light LED will light up immediately. When the button is pressed, the traffic light switches as programmed it before. If the order does not fit, check if the cables are connected to the correct pins of the Arduino.

The finished project in the overview:

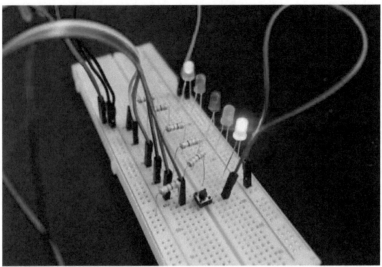

Figure 26 Structure of the finished project

Figure 27 Structure of the finished project

6.2. Control Servo Motor via Potentiometer

After we have mastered the control of LEDs, this example is about the control of motors. We distinguish between different classes of motors. There are motors that only need a supply voltage, e. g. DC motors, and there are motors that require additional hardware for control, e.g. stepper motors or brushless DC motors.

All these motors can be controlled and their speed adjusted by an Arduino. In this example we use a type of motor that is very often used in combination with an Arduino – the servo motor.

 A servo motor can determine the position of its shaft and can therefore be adjusted very precisely. This makes servo motors ideal for robotics projects, for example.

Unlike stepper motors, which can also be adjusted, servo motors are often less expensive and do not require any additional hardware.

The servo motor is controlled by the Arduino, the angular position of its shaft is determined by a rotary potentiometer.

6.2.1. Required Hardware

As always, we need a power supply. In our project, we will only control one servo motor, so the power supply via USB and the internal 5 V voltage converter of the Arduino is sufficient. If more than one servo motor is used in a project, an external power supply must be connected.

Purpose	Component
microcontroller	Arduino Uno REV 3
Power supply	USB cable
Actuator	MG90S servo motor
Position specification	B100kPotentiometer

Servo Motor

A servo motor is a DC motor with a built-in sensor. This determines the angular position of its motor shaft. In addition, the servo motor has a gear to increase the power or torque of the motor and to reduce the rotational speed.

For our project, we use an MG90S engine. This motor is almost identical in construction to the somewhat cheaper SG90 engine.

Figure 28 MG90S servo motor   *Figure 29 SG90 servo motor*

 The abbreviation MG in the servo designation stands for 'metal geared.' This means that the gear in the servo motor consists of metal gears and not of plastic gears, which are more susceptible to wear and tear. Therefore, MG motors allow for a significantly longer service life.

The position of the sensors can be adjusted from 0° to 180°. The motor is controlled by a pulse width modulated signal (PWM signal, see 5.3.4 analogWrite – PWM control)

Furthermore, the motors are supplied with 4.8 V - 6 V. The current consumption is 100 mA at 4.8 V. However, a servomotor can also absorb a considerably higher current for a short time period.

The servo motor has two pins for the supply voltage (Vcc and GND) and a signal pin that is connected directly to a digital output of the Arduino.

6.2.2. Programming

Theoretically, we could calculate which PWM signal belongs to which position of the servo. We would then have to generate a PWM signal and output it to the servomotor.

But often, there are pre-built libraries available that do just that.

Therefore, we use the library "Servo.h".

#include <Servo.h>

After we have included the library, we have to give our motor a name or declare it as an object in the program.

This is done before the setup part with

Servo servo1; // Create object

In the setup area, our servo is then assigned an output pin. In our example, it is assigned the digital output pin 2, which does not need to be declared as an output pin.

servo1.attach(2); // digital pin 2 – PWM signal for servo

Finally, we can specify the position of the servo motor with the function servo1.write(Position). The position must lie between 0° and 180°. servo1.write(80) sets the servo to 80°, for example.

Potentiometer

A potentiometer, often called a potentiometer for short, is a rotating resistor. Internally it consists of two adjustable resistors connected in series. By means of a sliding contact, either the upper or the lower resistance is increased. Correspondingly, the other resistance is decreased.

Figure 30 Potentiometer

The potentiometer has three connecting legs. Between the outer legs there is a permanent resistance of 100 kΩ. The resistance in the middle against the outer contacts depends on the position of the rotary wheel.

🔅 If we connect our supply voltage of 5 V to the external contacts, we get an adjustable voltage divider.
By turning the potentiometer, we can thus influence the ratio of the two resistance values and thus the voltage at the middle pin.

Lower position	Middle position	Upper position

6.2.3. Circuit Diagram

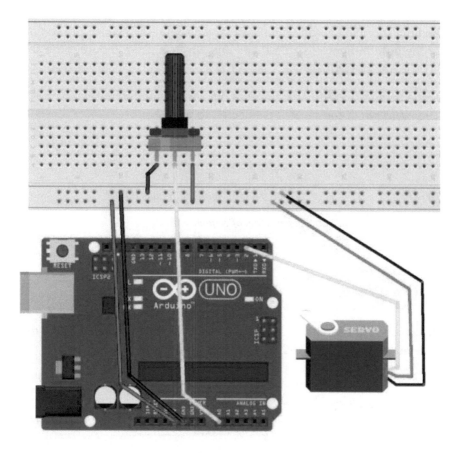

Figure 31 Circuit diagram

The circuit layout is kept very simple. The servo motor and the potenti-ometer are connected to the Arduino's power supply. The signal pin of the servo is connected to the digital pin 2 and the center of the potenti-ometer to the analog pin A0.

6.2.4. Programming

The programming is also kept very simple. First, the library is integrated and the servo initialized. Then, a variable is defined in which the voltage of the potentiometer is stored and one which is used to output the servo's degree position.

In the mandatory setup part, output pin 2 is assigned to the servo object. The PWM pin of the servo is connected to pin 2.

```
#include <Servo.h>

Servo servo1;                  // create object

int pot;                       // variable into which the voltage is read

int serv;           // Variable for output of degree

void setup() {

servo1.attach(2);   // digital pin 2 – PWM signal for servo

}
```

In the loop function, the voltage value is read in and rescaled into a degree number from 0 to 180. The position is then output.

```
void loop() {

pot = analogRead(A0);          // reads the analog value (0...1023)

serv = map(pot, 0, 1023, 0, 180);    // scaled to 180

servo1.write(serv);

delay(100);

}
```

A delay of 100ms at the end of the loop gives the servo enough time to take up the position before a new one is given.

Figure 32 Structure of the finished project

After the code has been uploaded to the Arduino, you can turn the potentiometer. The servomotor reacts to this by rotating as well.

Figure 33 Structure of the finished project

It looks as if the potentiometer and the servomotor are directly connected to each other, with the control being realized electronically via data processing in the Arduino.

6.3. Control Sensors – Weather Station

After we have built and programmed our first small projects, we are now moving on to a more extensive project.

The Arduino platform offers a wide range of sensors, some of which I would like to show you by way of example. In the exercise structure of this chapter, we will combine the control of different sensors and a display.

This example shows the construction and programming of a weather station.

The aim of the weather station is to measure temperature, humidity, brightness and soil moisture and to show them on a display. You will thus learn how to handle different sensors.

6.3.1. Required Hardware

The weather station must first be supplied with electrical energy. We will need a supply voltage, for example a 9 V power supply unit. The project would also be feasible with a power bank or block battery. In this example, we will use a 9 V block battery so that the station can also be operated wirelessly.

The first thing we need is, of course, an Arduino. We will use an Arduino Uno again, like we did in the previous examples. If you want to scale down the project, I recommend an Arduino Nano instead.

We also need the different sensors as well as some cables and our pegboard. Last but not least, we present the measured data on an OLED display.

Your First Projects

The following table shows the hardware used:

Purpose	Component
Microcontroller	Arduino Uno REV 3
Power supply	USB cable
Temperature and humidity	DHT22
Soil Moisture	Fire resistance
Brightness	Photo resistor
Rain detection	Rain sensor
Display	128x64 OLED display
Pulldown resistor	10 kΩ

Temperature and Humidity Sensor

There are many different ways to determine the temperature. A very in-expensive variant is a PTC or NTC resistor. A PTC (positive temperature coefficient) is a resistor whose resistance value increases with tempera-ture.

If we know the characteristic curve of the resistance according to the temperature, we can measure the resistance value to derive the temper-ature. The advantage of this measuring method is that a standard PTC costs merely a few cents. The disadvantage, on the other hand, is that you have to build a circuit for the measurement yourself. After all, the Arduino cannot read resistance values, but only voltage values. There-fore, you will need another resistor to build a voltage divider. The voltage dropping at the PTC is proportional to the resistance value of the PTC.

A simpler, but also more expensive method to measure the temperature are ready-made, intelligent modules. They measure the temperature, digitize it directly and send the data to the Arduino via an interface.

An example of such a device is the DHT22, a combined temperature and humidity sensor. It measures air temperature and relative humidity and transmits the values via the serial interface on request. This sensor is ideal for our project. It is capable of measuring both air humidity and temperature in one component.

The DHT22 is the "big brother" of the DHT11. They are mostly identical, only the accuracy is much better with the DHT22. The DHT22 has a temperature inaccuracy of 0.2 °C. With the DHT11 it is a whole 2 °C.

The cabling is also very simple. The sensor has four pins.

Alternatively, there are boards available that only lead out the three pins that are needed. One pin remains unused and has no function.

Figure 34DHT22 Sensor

The sensor design requires a supply voltage and a GND pin. There is also a pin to connect to a digital input pin of the Arduino.

Your First Projects

Programming the humidity sensor:

To program your humidity sensor, you first have to download the DHT library. As explained in chapter 5.1.3, search for the library via Tools -> Manage libraries.

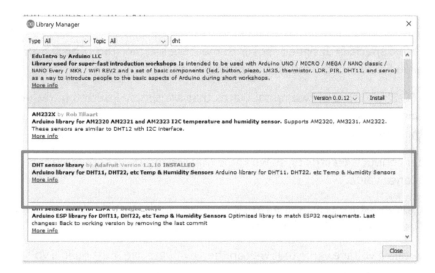

After the library has been installed, add it to the program code with

#include "DHT.h"

integrate.

The library is tailored to the DHT11 and DHT22 and offers simple functions to read humidity and temperature.

But first, we have to define which digital pin the sensor is connected to and which sensor it is. In our example we use a DHT22 on digital pin 2 of the Arduino.

DHT dht(2, DHT22);   //DigitalPin 2 and type DHT22

With the commands

dht.readTemperature() and dht.readHumidity() we can then easily read the temperature and humidity. In the program implemented, it will look like this:

```
float temp;              // Temperature in °C with decimal place

int humidity;            // relative humidity in whole %.

temp = dht.readTemperature();

humidity = dht.readHumidity();
```

Soil Moisture

We use a specially designed sensor to measure soil moisture. The sensor is called FC-28 and the measuring principle is kept simple.

The FC-28 consists of two metal plates that are simply inserted into the ground and have a high or low resistance towards each other depending on the humidity value.

Water conducts electricity, so we know that soil moisture depends on the resistance value.

The soil moisture sensor is a resistor whose conductivity is determined and dependent on the soil moisture.

To obtain a voltage value that we can then evaluate, we must build a voltage divider (2.5.1).

Example of a voltage divider:

We connect the sensor and a 100 kΩ resistor in series and tap at the center. This is how we measure the voltage across the resistor.

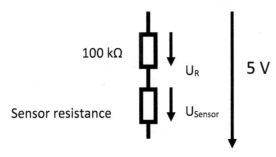

The following applies to the voltage at a voltage divider:

$$\frac{Voltage \ at \ resistor}{Total \ voltage} = \frac{Resistance \ value}{Total \ resistance}$$

$$Usensor = \frac{Sensor \ resistor}{Sensor \ resistor + 100k\Omega} \cdot 5V$$

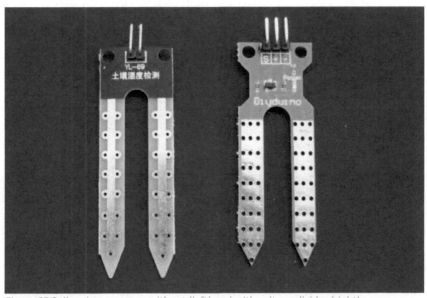

Figure 35 Soil moisture sensor without (left) and with voltage divider (right)

Alternatively, the same sensor is available with an integrated circuit board, in which a suitable voltage divider is already installed (right figure). Such "ready-to-go" sensors are recommended for beginners. The sensor has a Vcc-pin (supply voltage), a GND-pin and an analog output pin.

The advantage of the sensor used is that it converts the resistance value directly into a voltage of 0 V (corresponding to 0% soil moisture) up to a supply voltage of 5 V (corresponds to resistance-free, therefore conductive soil).

But for the schematic, the voltage divider is used. This enables you to build the circuit without such a ready-made module. The difference is only one more resistor on the plug-in board. The resistance value depends on the used module and lies within the range of 10 - 100 kΩ.

Programming of the soil moisture sensor:

Your First Projects

With our module, 0 V corresponds to a soil moisture of 0 % and 5 V corresponds to a soil moisture of 100 %. Read in analogously, this means that 0 % soil moisture corresponds to the value 0 and 100 % soil moisture corresponds to the value 1023.

 Depending on the sensor, it is possible that not the full value range is used. With the sensor used in our example, the value range does not reach a maximum of 1023, but only 878.

For a self-built voltage divider, you have to calculate the voltage range and thus the value range first.

With the map() command in conjunction with analogRead(), the result is a single command with five parameters.

```
int moisture;                // soil moisture in whole %

const int PIN_moisture = A0;   // analog input 0

Humidity = map(analogRead(PIN_moisture),0,878,0,100);
```

The variable moisture (soil moisture) is assigned the value read in from analog pin A0. This value (0...878) is previously converted into a percentage value (0...100). For more information about the map() function.

Light Sensor

To measure the brightness, we use a photo resistor. This resistor changes its value depending on the exposure intensity. The photo resistor has a resistance value of about 20 kΩ. If you illuminate it fully, for example with a flashlight, the resistor value is reduced to 100 Ω.

Analogously to the soil moisture sensor just discussed, which also creates a variable

Figure 36 Light resistance without (left) and with voltage divider (right)

resistance, a voltage divider must be set up for the light sensor, too.

There are, of course, ready-made sensor modules also in this area. Please note that the resistance decreases with much light, so the signal still has to be inverted.

Programming of the light sensor:

The programming corresponds exactly to that of the soil moisture sensor, only the value range was adjusted.

```
int brightness;              // brightness in whole percent

const int PIN_brightness = A1;    // analog input 1

brightness = map(analogRead(PIN_brightness),0,1023,100,0);
```

Rain Sensor

The rain sensor is the simplest in our example arrangement. We use a so-called FC-83 rain sensor (identical in construction to the YL-83 sensor).

There are only two track contacts. They have no connection, but can be short-circuited by a drop of water. If a connection is made between the contacts, there is water on the sensor. If the tracks are not connected, there is no water on the sensor.

Figure 37 Rain Sensor

Accordingly, we apply 5 V to one pin of the sensor and lead the other end to a digital input pin. If 5 V are also applied to this pin, we know that there is a connection, which means that it is raining.

We also need a pull-down resistor connected between the digital pin and the GND. This is necessary because the rain sensor is nothing more than a switch.

Programming of the rain sensor:

The digital pin is queried. If a connection exists, a HIGH is present and the word "yes" is stored in the variable *rain*. Otherwise, it does not rain and "no" is stored correspondingly.

```
const int PIN_rain = 3;        // digital pin 3

String rain;                    // rain yes or no


if (digitalRead(PIN_rain)) {

    rain = "yes";

}

else {

    rain = "no";

}
```

Display

The values that the sensors transmit to the controller are displayed on a 0.96-inch OLED display with 128x64 pixels.

The display communicates with the microcontroller via the I²C bus. For the I²C Bus, we need two lines. One line is used as clock input to specify when the data is transmitted. It is called SCL (serial clock). On the other line, the actual data is sent back and forth. This line has the abbreviation SDA (serial data).

The exact modeling and evaluation of the data on the I²C bus is less important for us. Let us thus concentrate on the control by existing libraries. We first have to connect the display. It has two pins for the supply voltage Vcc and GND as well as the two described data pins SCL and SDA.

 Different OLED displays from different manufacturers have different pin assignments. Vcc and GND are partially swapped. Always pay attention to the correct wiring!

The pins for the supply voltage are connected to the 5 V of the Arduino and ground via the plug-in board.

For a serial connection via I²C, the Arduino has the pins SDA and SCL to the left of the digital I/O pins.

Programming of the OLED display:

There are many different libraries for I²C displays. In the following, the "U8glib.h" library is used. It contains simple commands for displaying Latin letters, Arabic numerals and special characters. First, the library is installed via the library manager.

It is then called with

```
#include "U8glib.h"          // library for the display
```

loaded into the Arduino.

Next we have to tell the microcontroller that we have connected a display. We create an object with the command

```
U8GLIB_SH1106_128X64 oled(U8G_I2C_OPT_NONE);
```

Our display has been given the name "oled". "U8G_I2C_OPT_NONE" are the standard I²C options, but we will not go into further details about this.

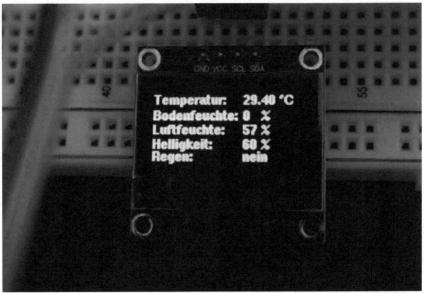

Figure 38 Data output (German) on the OLED display

The next step is to display the different variables and words. For this purpose, the following functions are available:

oled.firstPage();   Creates the "first page" of the display after program start

oled.nextPage();   Indicates whether a "next page" can be created. The two functions are used in combination to create a loop that constantly updates the display and overwrites the previous data.

oled.setFont(); Here you can set the text type, font size, etc.

oled.print();   prints a word or variable to the display

oled.write();   The same as oled.print for special characters

oled.setPrintPos(X, Y);   Sets a virtual cursor to the position (X|Y) (coordinates in pixels). The next character is printed at this position.

After we got to know the most important functions of the U8glib library, we can start programming.

For this purpose, we create a function Display_Output. As soon as this function is executed, the data is refreshed.

Your First Projects

Here is an example of the code for displaying the first line

```
void Display_Output() {

 oled.setFont(u8g_font_helvB08);   //font size 8, *bold* font

 oled.setPrintPos(0, 15);                // Sets the cursor to X=0, Y=15 pixels

  oled.print("Temperature: ");

 oled.setPrintPos(75, 15);               // Sets the cursor to X=75, Y=15 pixels

 oled.print(temp);            // Returns the content of the variable temp

  oled.setPrintPos(105, 15);

 oled.write(0xb0);            // Code for ° character

 oled.print("C");
```

We will go through the same procedure for all four lines.

In the main program (loop loop), we call the function.

```
The do-while loop executes the function until the function oled.nextPage(); returns an
error. This happens only in case of an error.

oled.firstPage();    // create first page

do {                            // execute ...

  Display_Output();

} while ( oled.nextPage() ); //... while the next page is "true".
```

6.3.2. Circuit Diagram

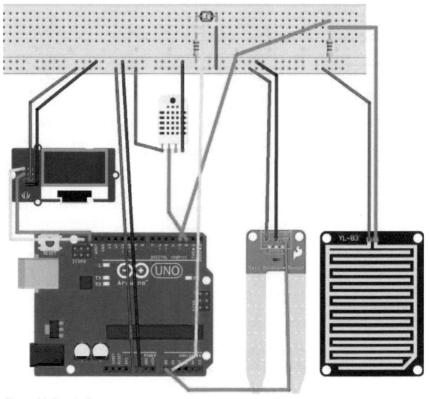

Figure 39 Circuit diagram

All modules are supplied with the 5V supply voltage.

The digital pin of the DHT22 module is connected to digital pin 2 of the Arduino.

The rain sensor is connected to the digital pin 3 of the Arduino via a 10 kΩ pull-down resistor.

The soil moisture sensor is connected to the analog input pin A0.

A voltage divider is built for the photo resistor. If a module with an integrated voltage divider is used, this resistor is not required. The tapped signal is fed in at analog pin A1.

6.3.3. Commitment Table

DHT22	Arduino Pin
Vcc (+)	5 V
GND (-)	GND
SIG (Do)	Pin 2

Soil Moisture Meter FC-28	Arduino Pin
Vcc (+)	5 V
GND (-)	GND
SIG (Do)	A0

Rain sensor FC-37	Arduino Pin
Pin 1 (+)	5 V
Pin 2 (-)	Pin 3

Photo sensor module	Arduino Pin
Vcc (+)	5 V
GND (-)	GND

SIG (Do)	A1

OLED display	Arduino Pin
Vcc (+)	5 V
GND (-)	GND
SCL	SCL
SDA	SDA

6.3.4. Programming

We have already broken down the programming of the individual sensors. In the following, the individual parts are combined to a coherent program. We always start by including the libraries. Next, we create objects for the display and for the DHT22 sensor. Finally, we define all variables and constants.

```
//////Weather station V1.2///////


#include "DHT.h"

#include "U8glib.h"                 // Library for the display

U8GLIB_SH1106_128X64 oled(U8G_I2C_OPT_NONE);     // Create the Display Object

DHT dht(2, DHT22);                  //DigitalPin 2 and type DHT22


float temp;            // Temperature in °C with decimal place

float temp; // Temperature in °C

int humidity; // relative humidity in %.
```

```
int moisture; // Soil moisture in %

int brightness; // brightness in %

String rain; // Rain Yes or No


const int PIN_rain = 3; // digital pin 3

const int PIN_moisture = A0; // analog input 0

const int PIN_brightness = A1; // analog input 1
```

Before we execute the setup(), the complete function Display_Output() is written.

```
void Display_Output() {

  oled.setFont(u8g_font_helvB08); //font size 8 and thick font

  oled.setPrintPos(0, 15); // Sets the cursor to X=0, Y=15 pixels

  oled.print("Temperature: ");

  oled.setPrintPos(75, 15); // Sets the cursor to X=75, Y=15 pixels

  oled.print(temp); // returns the content of the variable temp

  oled.setPrintPos(105, 15);

  oled.write(0xb0); // code for °-characters

  oled.print("C");

  // Output of soil moisture in line 2

  oled.setPrintPos(0, 28);

  oled.print("soil moisture:");

  oled.setPrintPos(75, 28);

  oled.print(moisture);

  oled.setPrintPos(90, 28);

  oled.print("%");

  // Output of humidity in line 3
```

```
oled.setPrintPos(0, 40);

oled.print("humidity:");

oled.setPrintPos(75, 40);

oled.print(humidity);

oled.setPrintPos(90, 40);

oled.print("%");

// Output of brightness in line 4

oled.setPrintPos(0, 52);

oled.print("brightness:");

oled.setPrintPos(75, 52);

oled.print(brightness);

oled.setPrintPos(90, 52);

oled.print("%");

// Output rain statuses in line 5

oled.setPrintPos(0, 62);

oled.print("Rain:");

oled.setPrintPos(75, 62);

oled.print(rain);

}
```

The setup part is kept very small. Only the digital input for the rain sensor is defined as INPUT and the communication to the DHT22 is set up with the command dht.begin().

```
void setup() {

dht.begin();

pinMode( PIN_rain, INPUT);

}
```

Your First Projects

In the main function, all sensor data are read in and converted. In the next step, the function Display_Output() is executed to display the data on the OLED display.

```
void loop() {

  if (digitalRead(PIN_rain)) { // if it rains the pin is HIGH

    rain = "yes";

  }

  else {

    rain = "no";

  }

  //Convert the sensor value (0...878) in percent (0..100)//

  moisture = map(analogRead(PIN_moisture), 0, 878, 0, 100);

  //Convert the sensor value (0...1023) to percent (0..100)//

  brightness = map(analogRead(PIN_brightness), 0, 1023, 100, 0);

  temp = dht.readTemperature();

  humidity = dht.readHumidity();


  oled.firstPage(); //create first page

  do { //execute....

    Display_Output();

  } while ( oled.nextPage() ); //... while the next page is "true

  delay(60000); // One minute time delay

}
```

Since a measurement is to be made once per minute, a 'delay' of 60,000 milliseconds (60 seconds) at the end of the loop provides the corresponding time delay.

Theoretically, we would have to subtract the time the microcontroller needs to execute the remaining commands. But this is only a fraction of a second.

The program is uploaded again using the arrow in the upper left corner.

After the program has been successfully uploaded, the OLED display shows the values of temperature, soil moisture, humidity and brightness as well as the rain status. Once per minute, the measured values are read in again and shown on the display.

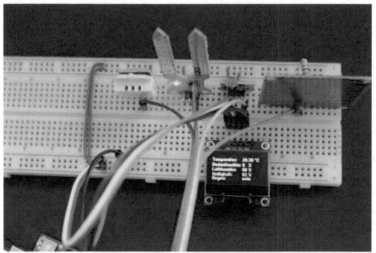

Figure 40 Structure of the finished project

Figure 41 Structure of the finished project

Your First Projects

7. The Most Common Beginners' Mistakes

No master has ever fallen from heaven. Everybody makes mistakes, especially if you are new to something. However, the advantage of a guidebook like this one is that you can learn from the mistakes of others without having to make them yourself. This is why we go through the most common beginners' mistakes, both in terms of software and hardware.

7.1. Short Circuits, Smoke, Heat

If something starts to get hot or even starts smoking, the power supply must be removed immediately. The cause is most probably a short circuit, for example because the pins for the power supply have been swapped (Vin or 5 V and GND). Check all connections to see if there is a short circuit somewhere. It might also happen because you have connected two rows on the board unplanned. The connection diagram of the pinboard 3.7 helps to check this.

Selecting a series resistor in an LED or transistor that is too small can also produce a possible heat source. If all cables have been checked for short circuits, a defective component might be the source of the heat development. However, it is advisable to analyze the wiring and the circuit diagram in detail to see if there is a planning error, so as not to 'sacrifice' further components.

7.2. Controller Crashes – Faulty Components

If the Arduino controller crashes, this is usually because the power supply has dropped. Check your power supply and see if the power supply is of high quality and able to deliver enough power. If the Arduino is powered by a powerbank or a block battery, check if the charge level is sufficient.

When connecting via USB, it can happen that the voltage drops because the USB port is too weak and the cables are too long.

On the other hand, a load problem might be affecting the voltage and cause it to drop. For example, if motors are used, they can draw a relatively large amount of current when starting up and the power supply will fail as a result.

The recommended solution is to replace the power supply with a high-quality power supply unit. For projects with many loads (e. g. motors), you should always connect an additional power supply. Each Arduino-Shield for larger projects has input sockets for an external power supply.

If components do not function properly or fail completely, it may be because they are supplied with too much or too little voltage. A look at the specifications will help. Mostly the components are operated with 3.3 V or 5 V. In addition, when powering the devices with more than 5 V, you have to take care not to use the vin-pin for powering the components, because it is directly connected to the input socket.

7.3. Bus Communication Failure

You might be using an I²C display, but communication does not work. The I²C bus needs two pull-up resistors for SDA and SCL. They are usually integrated directly at the components (e. g. the display). In case of long lines, several consumers on the bus or an unstable power supply, it might help to switch two 4.7 kΩ resistors from SDA and SCL against 5 V.

7.4. LED Is Not Lit

If a LED should light up but does not, the cause might be a hardware or software error. The LED is probably installed incorrectly (positive pole to the longer leg) or the series resistor is too big. It is important to consider how much voltage and current the LED needs.

On the other hand, if the series resistance is too low, the LED might overheat and burn out, so to speak.

If none of these causes apply, there must be a software error. The digital OUTPUT may have been declared as INPUT by mistake, the wrong pin may have been specified, or a program error might prevent the digital pin from being activated.

7.5. No Such File or Directory

```
#include "DHT.h"
#include "U8glib.h"
U8GLIB_SH1106_128X64 oled(U8G_I2C_OPT_NONE);
DHT dht(2, DHT22);
```

```
DHT.h No such file or directory
exit status 1
DHT.h: No such file or directory
```

Illustration 42 Error No such file or directory

With this error, the library to be included is missing. In the example above, the library DHT.h is not available and must be installed first. See 5.1.3 Add libraries.

7.6. Expected ';' Before 'Token'

```
const int PIN_gruenA = 3;
const int PIN_schalter = 2


void setup()
{
    //Definiere Als In- und Outputs
```

```
expected ',' or ';' before 'void'


exit status 1
expected ',' or ';' before 'void'
```

Figure 43 Error Expected ',' or ';' before 'void'

This error indicates that a semicolon is missing after a statement. Usually the problem lies just above the line that was marked red. In the example above, the semicolon is missing after

const int PIN_schalter = 2;

100

7.7. Expected Initializer Before '...'

This error, or often also *expect `}' at end of input* occurs often if you are new to programming.

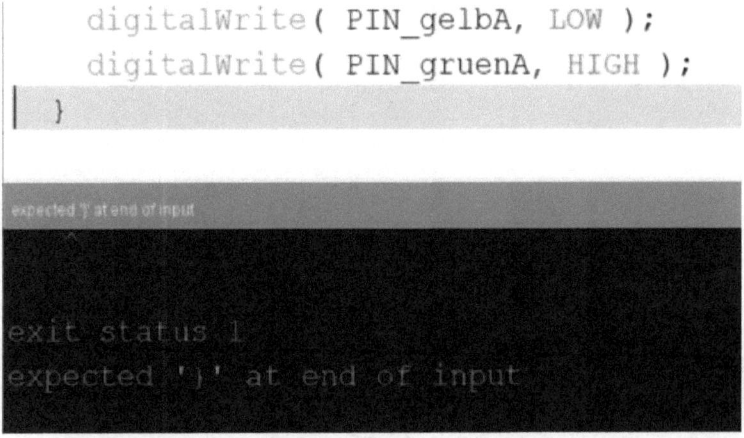

```
digitalWrite( PIN_gelbA, LOW );
digitalWrite( PIN_gruenA, HIGH );
}
```

```
expected '}' at end of input


exit status 1
expected '}' at end of input
```

Figure 44 Error Expected '}' at end of input

If one of these errors appears, a curly bracket is missing somewhere. For each open brace, there must always be a closed brace.

7.8. Expected Declaration Before '...' Token

```
digitalWrite( PIN_gruenA, HIGH );
}
}
}
```

```
expected declaration before '}' token


exit status 1
expected declaration before '}' token
```

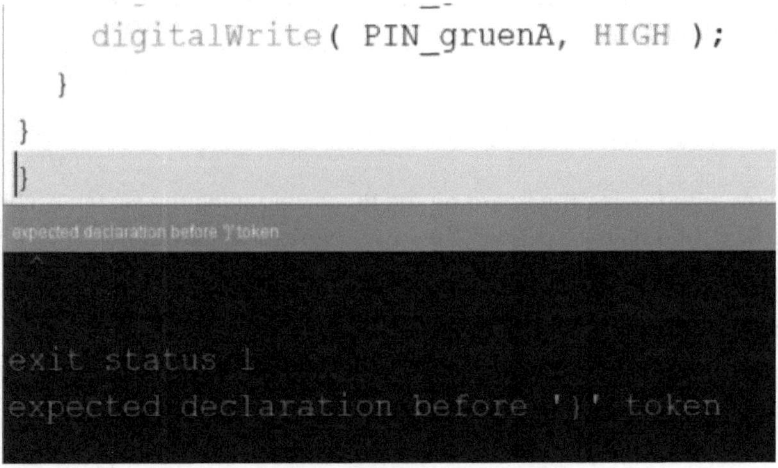

Figure 45 Error Expected declaration before '}'

On the other hand, this error message appears if one curly bracket is superfluous.

Formatting also helps here for verification. In the beginning, correct stapling is tedious, but you will get used to it over time.

See also the formatting help 5.2 Indenting.

7.9. Redefinition of '...'

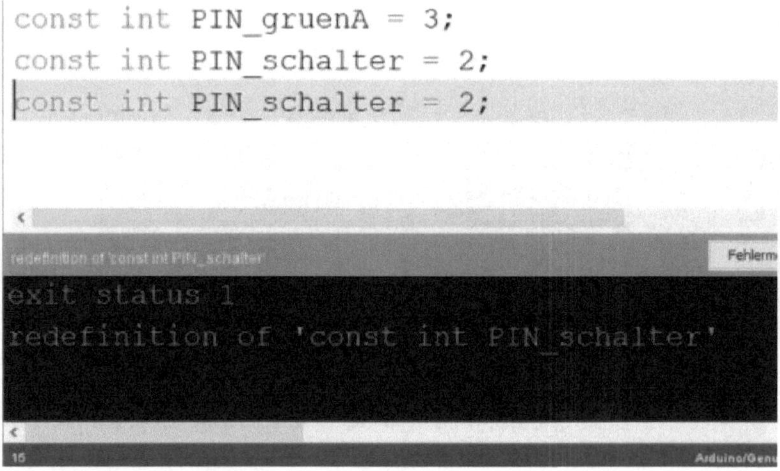

```
const int PIN_gruenA = 3;
const int PIN_schalter = 2;
const int PIN_schalter = 2;
```

redefinition of 'const int PIN_schalter'   Fehlerm

exit status 1
redefinition of 'const int PIN_schalter'

16   Arduino/Genu

Figure 46 Error Redefinition of '...'

Something was defined multiple times, although it may only occur once. This error can easily happen if you add foreign lines of code to a program using copy and paste.

7.10. Problem Uploading to Board

Problems with finding the board on the PC or uploading the sketch occur often. First, you have to check if the PC recognizes the Arduino.

To do this, open the Device Manager under Windows and see if the Arduino is recognized under the COM & LPT ports.

The Most Common Beginners' Mistakes

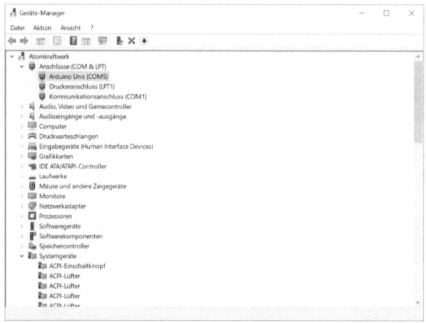

Figure 47 Windows Device Manager

If the Arduino is recognized, this is a good sign. If a COM port is recognized when the Arduino is plugged in, but it is not called an Arduino, the appropriate drivers are most likely missing. This happens frequently with Arduino clones. In this case, the drivers can be found on the manufacturers' websites.

If no COM port is detected, there may be a hardware defect. First, however, it is recommended to change the USB cable; because often the USB cables are not shielded sufficiently or of poor quality. Changing the USB cable may solve the problem. If an Arduino clone is used, suitable drivers may have to be installed first.

After the Arduino is recognized, the correct port and board must be selected in the Arduino IDE.

If the Arduino is recognized and can be selected, but the sketch cannot be uploaded, another program may access the serial port and block it.

The Most Common Beginners' Mistakes

Figure 48 Error Problem while uploading to the board

This error becomes noticeable by the error "can't open device." It is recommended to close all other programs if this issue occurs.

These were the most common mistakes when using Arduino. If you encounter an error that is not listed here, the Arduino forum https://forum.arduino.cc/ or the WorldWideWeb can certainly help.

In general, the official Arduino website offers a lot of help. In addition, many projects and tutorials can be found online.

Free eBook

Thanks for buying this book. Since the printing of the book is done directly by Amazon and I have no influence on the quality of the pictures and formatting. It is possible that some details are lost.

For this reason, I offer the eBook as a PDF file (and source codes of the examples) free of charge when you buy the book. There, all pictures are high resolution and you always get the latest version.

To download your eBook, send a message with the subject line "Free Arduino-eBook" as well as a screenshot of the purchase or proof of order from Amazon to this email address:

Benjamin-Spahic@web.de

I will send you the eBook and the program codes for the projects immediately.

If you are missing something, did not like something or have suggestions for improvement or questions, please feel free to send me an e-mail.

Constructive criticism is important to be able to improve something. I am constantly revising the book and am happy to respond to any constructive suggestions for improvement.

Otherwise, if you liked the book, I would also appreciate a positive review on Amazon. This helps increase the book's visibility and is the biggest praise an author can get.

Yours truly,

Benjamin

About the Author

Benjamin Spahic was born in Heidelberg, Germany, in 1995 and grew up in a village of 8,000 souls near Karlsruhe. His passion for technology is reflected in his studies of electrical engineering with a focus on information technology at the University of Applied Sciences in Karlsruhe.

Afterwards, he deepened his knowledge in the field of regenerative energy production at the University of Applied Sciences Karlsruhe for Technology and Economics.

Free eBook

Legal Notice:

Author: Benjamin Spahic

Address:
Benjamin Spahic

Konradin-Kreutzer-Str. 12

76684 Oestringen

Proofreading/Editing: Oliver Nova

Proofreading US Version: Mentorium GMBH

Cover: Kim Nusko

ISBN: 9798551464921

Email: Benjamin-Spahic@web.de

Facebook: Benjamin Spahic

Arduino Without Prior Knowledge

First release 21.10.2020

Distribution through kindledirectpublishing

Amazon Media EU S.à r.l., 5 Rue Plaetis, L-2338, Luxembourg

Free eBook

Picture Credits:

All contents not mentioned above were created by the author himself. He is, therefore, the author of the graphics and has the rights of use and distribution.

Illustration 1*: https://commons.wikimedia.org/wiki/File:Z3_Deutsches_Museum.JPG

Illustration 3*: https:
//de.wikipedia.org/wiki/Datei:Widerst%C3%A4nde.JPGFigure 4**: https://de.wikipe-dia.org/wiki/Datei:Resistor_symbol_America.svg

Illustration 6**: https://de.wikipedia.org/wiki/Datei:Diodenalt2.png

Illustration 8*: https://de.wikipedia.org/wiki/Datei:Diode_pinout_de.svg

Illustration 10*: https://de.wikipedia.org/wiki/Datei:Elko-Al-Ta-Bauformen-Wiki-07-02-11.jpg

Illustration 11*: https://commons.wikimedia.org/wiki/File:Kondensatoren-Schaltzeichen-Reihe.svg

Illustration 15**:https://commons.wikimedia.org/wiki/File:AVR_group.jpg

Illustration 16**:https://commons.wikimedia.org/wiki/File:ArduinoUnoSMD.jpg

Illustration 17**: https://de.wikipedia.org/wiki/Datei:Arduino_uno_r3_isometr.jpg

Illustration 18**:https://commons.wikimedia.org/wiki/File:ArduinoUnoSMD.jpg

Illustration 19**: https://store.arduino.cc/arduino-uno-rev3

Made in United States
Troutdale, OR
09/19/2023

13002829R00066